Plant Spirit Wisdom

Sin Eaters and Shamans:

The Power of Nature in

Celtic Healing for the Soul

First published by O-Books, 2008
Reprinted, 2011
O-Books is an imprint of John Hunt Publishing Ltd., Laurel House, Station Approach,
Alresford, Hants, SO24 9JH, UK
office1@o-books.net
www.o-books.com

For distributor details and how to order please visit the 'Ordering' section on our website.

Text copyright: Ross Heaven 2008

ISBN: 978 1 84694 123 8

A CIP catalogue record for this book is available from the British Library.

Design: Stuart Davies

Printed in the UK by CPI Antony Rowe
Printed in the USA by Offset Paperback Mfrs, Inc

We operate a distinctive and ethical publishing philosophy in all
areas of our business, from our global network of authors to
production and worldwide distribution.

Plant Spirit Wisdom

Sin Eaters and Shamans:

The Power of Nature in

Celtic Healing for the Soul

Ross Heaven

BOOKS

Winchester, UK
Washington, USA

CONTENTS

Here, where the loves of others close
The vision of my heart begins
The wisdom that within us grows
Is absolution for our sins

Faith by George William Russell ('A. E.')

FOREWORD

There is much that we in the modern world can learn from our tribal ancestors. Their understanding of the beneficial properties of the natural world was vast. Where ancient tribes have survived alongside the prehistoric landscapes which nurtured them, we are anxious to conserve this exotic knowledge and to learn from it. The devastating rate at which these peoples and pockets of prehistoric life are being destroyed is highlighting the urgent need to protect those that remain. Thankfully, growing concern is revealing much ancient wisdom that has previously been unappreciated. Even so plants, creatures and even tribes of humans are still discovered only to become extinct soon after.

Trees and herbs have always been of paramount importance to ancient wisdom. We know for example that the trees of the tropical rainforest yield valuable medicines familiar for thousands of years to the indigenous peoples but only recently discovered by modern science. Strangely we don't seem to place the same value on our own inherited wisdom. Tribal wisdom is often forgotten as land use changes. Homelands are mined, forested or farmed or put to some other wholesale commercial use. Rivers are dammed and valleys flooded. Wars tear nations apart and nomadic peoples become urbanised. Ancient woods are ripped up and lakes are drained. Amongst all this chaos, plant communities and creatures dependent upon old ways of living still cling to life. There is best hope for their survival where the traditions of the people survive, which for centuries have shaped the environment.

When the Romans invaded Great Britain nearly two thousand years ago in 43 CE, they found a land peopled by individual tribes who were collectively known as the Celts. Although these Celtic tribes had no central government or overall leader, they shared many common beliefs. Ancestral reverence and a firm belief in the afterlife formed the foundation of their spirituality. They lived in harmony with the natural world and believed that the spirit behind creation was in all things and that all things in nature had something valuable to teach humankind.

The Celtic tribes had travelled far in their search for freedom. They revered many deities, above all the White Goddess, and had a vast storehouse of wisdom about the human relationship with the natural world. The well-being of the tribe depended on the well-being of nature and since trees had so much to offer, they were held in very high esteem. Each species of tree and plant had its own particular treasures to offer in terms of shelter, energy, food and medicine. Their location, nature and habit were of sacred significance in the arts of healing, magic and spirituality. This was true of all things in nature.

The Celts believed that we, and all other things, are all an important part of the Universal Order. There is no escaping the consequences of our decisions and actions in the never-ending cycle of life and rebirth. Whatever we do inevitably affects everything else that might happen on all levels of existence, physical, mental and spiritual. We must all take individual responsibility for our deeds and intentions.

Specially trained elders, both men and women, committed the history and knowledge of their tribe to memory and passed it down in verse through the generations. They were master poets and magicians who commanded enormous respect among their peoples. Poetry was then the most revered and also feared of all the creative arts. Training was long and immensely complex and took a minimum of twelve years to complete. Symbolism and association were the keys to the wisdom of the Celts, but since theirs was largely an oral tradition unlocking their secrets has always proved difficult.

The Celtic world view was outlawed in mainland Europe and Britain in the wake of Roman domination. Because all of Ireland, the Isle of Man and the remotest parts of Scotland, Wales, Cornwall and Brittany escaped Roman influence for much longer than most of the rest of Europe, the ways of the ancient Celtic tribes have been best preserved here and the landscape is still shaped by traditional farming and forestry, although a great many of the native trees have gone and been replaced by sheep and plantation pines. Ancient customs are still reflected in plant communities which have been shaped by centuries of partnership with our ancestors on old pasture, in orchards, woodland, hedge and heath, on our shores and mountainsides, in our skies, in our rivers and lakes and the sea.

After contending with two thousand years of religious persecution, the ways of our ancient Celtic ancestors still survive today in the memories of the master poets and in the actions of those who persist in the Old Ways. It is found in place names and in the common names of plants, even in the names of Saints. Where the Roman church could not suppress old beliefs and customs it renamed festival days and adopted old gods like Brigid and Green George as Saints and gave their acts a Christian spin. Ancient herbal remedies continue to work, like willow, for colds and fevers engendered by damp, now the familiar *Aspirin*. New ones are discovered, like *Taxol*, a possible cure for cancer, isolated from yew. Traditional trades and farming practices still draw on our ancestors' vast knowledge of working with the natural world so that resources are endless. Tribal stories persist in myths and festivals, in customs, songs and superstitions

The ancient Celts left few written records save for mysterious runes known as Ogham. Many centuries of study have revealed some of their magic, but there is little we can be certain of when interpreting what remains of ancient Celtic wisdom. We don't know how to pronounce old Gaelic, let alone how to translate it. Collections of Celtic mythology like the thirteenth Century *Red Book of Hergest* or the romances of medieval Brittany give us some clues, but such records have often been revised to suit the mood of the times or deliberately jumbled to confuse all but the most learned scholars and poets. Some are simply frauds. Among academics there is little agreement. Robert Graves' twentieth century classic, *The White Goddess*, is a masterwork to some and incomprehensible rubbish to others.

We can only paint a picture of the wisdom of the ancient Celts in the broadest strokes. If in doing this we reawaken a deeper respect for the wonder and resourcefulness of the natural world and the lessons to be learned from every part of it, then it is worth doing. Science has become conceited. We now aim to change and predict Nature's design on a global scale. We forget that life on this planet is far bigger than us and inextricably connected to the rhythm of the seasons and the movement of the planets.

As Earth changes on a cosmic scale, species come and go in the blink of an eye. Every part is interconnected and we are each vital in the enormous mysteries of space and time. Getting to know yourself was one of the keys to ancient Celtic wisdom. By focussing first on living happily with ourselves, perhaps we could learn to live in peace with each other.

Jane Gifford is the author of *The Celtic Wisdom of Trees*, published in UK by Godsfield Press 2000 and 2006, and in USA by Sterling as *The Wisdom of Trees*

INTRODUCTION

THE REWORLD

It would be an ill thing if wonders were for the seeing
And we without the seeing them.
**Pwyll, Prince of Dyfed, in *The Fates of the Princes of Dyfed* by
Kenneth Morris**

Plants have always held a special fascination for me, for their symbolic and spiritual qualities, and for the healing they bring.

On the day I was born, so family legend goes, a Romany woman called at our house, as they did in those days, selling lucky heather door-to-door. She looked down at me sleeping, then at my mother, and said, "He'll be a healer when he grows, and, if God smiles on him, maybe a poet. Tell him to remember me in his words."

Flattery will get you everywhere, it seems, and, for those few kind words, my mother gave her sixpence, and hung the heather over my crib.

When I was eight, we moved deeper into nature, to the countryside on the borders of Wales, and according to another family legend, I fell in love – with a holly tree.

I spent hours admiring it, befriending it, and braving the glossy hard spikes of its leaves to crawl beneath its canopy so I could sit with my back to its trunk. Inside its prickly evergreen cape I felt peaceful, protected, and safe.

Holly is not a plant much recommended by herbalists; its berries are violently purgative and its leaves, while being of some use to patients with catarrh and jaundice, are so sour that the disease is almost preferable to the cure. But its spirit is strong and comforting, and it was much favoured by the Druids and healers of Wales.

Of course, I knew none of that then. But I loved it all the same.

Years later, after my infatuation with the holly was over and I had turned my attention to human females, my first child was conceived.

I had a vision of her, my daughter, at the moment of conception, running down a hillside in summer towards me, her arms full of yellow flowers as her gift to me for bringing her into the world. Four years later, on a hillside in Sussex, my vision came true, and there she was, just as I'd seen her, in a pretty floral dress, with white-blonde hair, a wide smile, and golden flowers in her arms; all of it just as I'd seen. "These are for you, daddy," she said, "Thank you." And then she ran off.

She never told me what she was thanking me for, but I knew.

Now my children are grown and, on winter nights, when the fog drifts in from the bay, I sometimes accept the invitation of the mist, as the Celts so often did in their stories of the fey, and step for a moment into the otherworld, the place we go when our time on Earth is done.

It is as well to know the terrain, and I am quite familiar with that landscape now.

I wonder, when it is my time, if old souls will visit me, as they are said to do, to guide us on our final journeys, and will they also bring flowers? It would be appropriate, since flowers are often the gifts of spirits and of mortals when endings come to pass and *"The Great Spirit whose home is in the vast becomes for us a moving glamour in the heavens."** – and since my life began with heather.

We are some years from that happy departure, however, and so while we share this time together, let us turn our attention to the story of this book. It began, I am tempted to say, in the 1970s, in the county of Herefordshire, in the heart of England, where I was fortunate enough to meet and work with a sin eater – a Celtic healer and "devourer of human sins" – who was also a practitioner of folk healing and spiritual herbalism.

My meeting with this man, Adam, led to a friendship or, I

---

* George William Russell, in *The Candle of Vision: Inner Worlds of the Imagination*

suppose, a sort of informal apprenticeship, which lasted more than ten years. During this time, I learned some of the Celtic arts of healing, the spiritual properties of plants, herbs, and trees, and the wisdom of nature. I also came to understand the meanings and methods of sin and how to care for the soul. It is these things that I wish to share with you.

To say that our journey begins in the 1970s is not entirely true, however. Like all things, our story really starts thirteen billion years ago, somewhere deep in the darkness of space. At that time, hydrogen and helium were all there was to the universe, and you and I were a distant dream. Nevertheless, the universe *did* dream and from this came the birth of stars.

Following this 'Big Bang', carbon, oxygen, and iron, the heavier elements, were created; cooked up in the furnace-hearts of stars until, some billions of years later, they expanded, exploded, and became supernovas, throwing their elements out into space, like seeds on a cosmic wind.

These seed-clouds collapsed too, forming new communities of attraction and similarity: second-generation stars and planets. And, with that, our lives began.

We are made from stardust, you and I. A star had to be born for the carbon, oxygen, and iron in our bodies to exist, and it had to die for us to live. We share our origins and our elements with every life form on our planet and with everything that is. We are all born of stars and to them we will return. It is just a matter of time.

The universe is still expanding from that first great spark of life all those billions of years ago, and it will do so until there is no more energy to sustain it or the life it has created in its flow, and then it will end. For a while, all that will be left of us will be the faintest glimmer of radiance from our departed souls. And then the process will begin again and we will be reborn as infant stars. Back to their luminous hearts is where evolution and our destinies take us.

I love that vision of the universe: human beings emerging from stars and blazing our paths on Earth until we shine so brightly that God cannot help but notice us and make new stars of us. Our journeys create the perfect circle and give meaning to our lives, solving in the process one of the greatest riddles of existence: Why are we here?

Simple. We are creatures of fire and light, here to burn as brightly as we can until we return to the womb of the universe which held us first when we were light and longing, aching to be born.

In the words of the 13th century mystic and poet, Jalalludin Rumi:

We come spinning out of nothingness
Scattering like stars.

THE THREE SHOUTS OF GOD

Long before our scientists created this romantic drama of the heavens, the Celts had a view of creation and human purpose which is in many ways similar. In the beginning, they said, Three Shouts were sent out into the world when God (who is evolving as we are) became conscious, aware, and spoke His name into the Void [1]. With that, all things were created in the great music of His voice and His song of new awareness: "I Am That".

Within this sound was light, and within this light was form, and this was the birth of all life [2]. It was also the death of God. For, in creating life, 'God' ceased to be and took shape instead in the plants, animals, stones, trees, waves of the shore, men and women, and all the Kingdoms of the world.

We became God on Earth, so that He and we might explore, adventure, and discover our meanings together.

The great Welsh poet, Taliesin, captures the essence of this God-in-all-things and of man-as-God in these lines from the *Mabinogion*, the first book of Celtic myths:

I was in many forms
before I was set free...
I believe, when I was formed
I was teardrops in the air

I was a star-woven star
I was the truth of a letter
I was the tale of origins
I was illuminated lanterns…

I have been all men known to history
Wondering at the world and at time passing;
I have seen evil, and the light blessing
Innocent love under a spring sky…

King, beggar and fool, I have been all by turns
Knowing the body's sweetness, the mind's treason;
Taliesin still, I show you a new world, risen
Stubborn with beauty, out of the heart's need.

Because of the power of the word, no-one should ever pronounce
God's name aloud, but it is known. It was presented to Celtic seers
as three letters, each like a ray of the sun; one signifying the dawn,
the new day rising; a vertical line for the high sun at noon; and a
third for the sweet peace of evening. God is the sun, for he, too,
was born of a star.

These three letters have sounds: O, I, and W, the Bardic name for
God. If it were ever to be spoken (which it must not, for who
knows what act of creation might result), it would be pronounced
as O-EE-OO. Sounding it out in your mind, the song of God
becomes a wail of self-awareness, a melancholy keening like a
newborn might make. This cry of awakening into the wilderness of
non-existence was the beginning of all things.

Whichever version of creation you prefer, the scientist's Big
Bang or the poet's Great Song of Being, it is still only half the story.
It tells us how the universe came to be, but not what it is or what
our role within it might be.

A reporter once asked Albert Einstein about this. What, he wanted to know, was the most important question facing humanity. I imagine he expected an answer like "Why are we here?" or, in a time of atom bombs and political chill, "How to ensure world peace". Einstein thought about it and then replied: "Is the universe a friendly place?"

It is a question we are still asking, and we all must answer it for ourselves.

It is important to do so, and to find the right solution, for if we decide that the universe is unfriendly or has no meaning, we will do all in our power to destroy it and ourselves along with it. If we decide that it is friendly, we will greet it joyfully and learn from it to embrace life and create a home here for ourselves. It is the difference between seeing God in all things, as Taliesin did, and turning our backs on God and our star-bound destinies.

The physicist, Dr Brian Cox, has one answer to Einstein's question:

> Even if the universe is fundamentally meaningless,
> human beings are the sparks of meaning within it.

Rumi has another:

> Love is the order of the universe
> And we are its atoms.

We *are* the universe and we give it meaning. By its very nature, therefore, it can mean us no harm – unless we mean to harm ourselves.

It is true that the world can appear unfathomable, or full of anger and hurt. But still we must choose to see the world ensouled and full of love and hope, because it will respond to our choices and create for us what we see.

The ability to make wise choices is so important that the Celtic seers developed skills for travelling between worlds to meet with God and know His purpose. Then, like Prometheus, they brought their secrets and answers back to inform our actions and light our way on Earth.

The first of these travellers between worlds were the *Gwynfydolion*; those who lived in the Circle of Blessedness. When God spoke His name, they awoke first.

"We are serpents," they said. "Lucifers. And we blaze a path between Infinity [*Ceugant*] and the physical world [*Abred*]." ('Lucifers' literally means 'Light-bringers' or 'Angels of Light'.)

From the *Gwynfydolion* the first knowledge came of the plants, the spirit, and the means of inspiration. Through their teachings, others awoke and learned these skills as well. They were the Bards (inspired poets), Druids (priests, healers, and magicians), and Ovates (omen-readers and future-seers); all of them serpents too.

Snakes and dragons have always been the symbols and allies of wise men and healers. The emblem of Wales is the dragon, God is The Blazing Dragon of Wisdom, and the priests of Wales were initiated in caves, the lairs of dragons.

In Ireland, too, the snake is an ancient symbol of the sacred. Legend has it that in the 5th century, Saint Patrick drove the serpents from the land, using his staff to herd them into the sea and banish them for eternity. The Irish lament that, since this time, their knowledge of nature, healing, and the truths of the spirit began to disappear.

The Scottish Celts also knew of the connections between serpents, healing, and wisdom. In the town of Callander Lowland, there is a high mound, made by men, in a serpentine form, to honour the power and spirit of the Earth. It makes its way from the dry land to the river, the waters of inspiration.

Mythologists like Joseph Campbell tell us that wherever nature and the awakened self is venerated, the serpent appears in the myths and culture of the people. It is a symbol of the Divine, like nature itself, and all that is required of us in order to know God is for us to notice the serpent in the Garden and accept his invitation to eat from the Tree of Knowledge.

Then we will know that God is all there is and We Are That.

THE HEALING WORK OF THE SIN EATER

The Welsh word *adfyd* means 'Reworld' and refers to this state of vision and grace, where we become aware, ecstatically, of the presence of God in every aspect of our lives.

Our spiritual evolution towards this grace may take several lifetimes, as we cast off the illusions we have been born to and come to see our lives and place in the universe for what they really are. Fortunately, we have these lifetimes available to us, since the universe will not end tomorrow.

Reincarnation is a hardship in Celtic philosophy, however. We might even say it is a punishment for our sins, and for one sin in particular: the Original (that is, *Origin*-al) Sin of forgetting our beginnings as the star-children of God and becoming lost in the world of illusions. Original Sin is a refusal to reworld and take our rightful place.

The individual charged with responsibility for removing these sins and bringing our souls back to balance and understanding was the sin eater.

Perhaps because sin eating is a lost tradition, or because sin eaters did not have a formal title like Druid, Bard, or Ovate, little is really known of them, and I can only tell you about the one I met.

Adam had the inspired, poetic, and philosophical skills of the Bard and story-teller, his teachings an appeal to the soul more than to reason, since life's truths are better understood in metaphor and symbol than in cold data and hard 'fact'. He was also a seer who knew how to 'read' nature for guidance and signs of the future. More especially, he was a healer of the soul and knew its wounds.

One of the better-known (or at least, more visible) aspects of a sin eater's work was his employment at funerals to eat a last meal from the belly of a corpse as it lay in state. By so doing he would absorb the sins of the dead and restore the soul to balance so that the deceased would have passage to the next world.

John Aubrey, writing in 1688, describes the ritual in Hereford and Wales:

The manner was that when a Corpse was brought out of the

house and laid on the Bier; a Loaf of bread was brought out and delivered to the Sin-eater over the corps, as also a Mazer-bowl full of beer, which he was to drink up, and sixpence in money, in consideration whereof he took upon him all the Sins of the Defunct, and freed him (or her) from Walking after they were dead. [5]

What is less well-known about sin eaters is that they did not just work with the dead. Many of them, because of their rural location and closeness to nature, were also skilled in folk medicine, a form of 'root doctoring' or herbalism, which works with the medicinal properties and more importantly, the spiritual essence of plants.

This was certainly the case for Adam, who was a gifted spiritual herbalist and a 'cunning man' who worked extensively with plants to cure those who came for healing.

One of his favourites was the nettle. On the face of it, it is difficult to see how nettles – commonly regarded as weeds, if they're regarded by us at all – could justify the words of constant praise he lavished on them. "They are the finest healers on our planet," he would say.

Nettles have many medicinal uses, however, some of which we are only just discovering. Adam knew them all, without the aid of scientific tests or formal education, 40 years ago.

His knowledge and healing methods were inspired rather than rational and would best be described as 'folk medicine' (and dismissed by sceptics on that basis alone), yet modern trials tend to prove that the qualities and attributes he saw in nettles are exactly as he related them. He taught that they were good for the the kidneys, bladder, circulation, and the heart, and indeed, they are now recommended for these very purposes.

Other studies show that flogging with nettles (*urtication*) – which Adam himself practiced – provides relief for rheumatism. Nettle extract can also be used to treat arthritis and anemia. Adam maintained that nettles were excellent for the blood, and this proves to be the case as well. The fresh leaves will stop all types of bleeding due to their high content of vitamin K, while the dried plant is used to thin the blood.

When I would ask him how he knew these things, he would use words I have subsequently heard from many shamans and plant healers in countries as remote from one another as Eire and Peru: "I asked them and their spirits were gracious enough to tell me."

It was not just the physical characteristics of nettles that interested Adam, however. He believed that they, like us, have a soul, an evolutionary destiny, and a spiritual and healing intention. It was their love that really healed.

The spirit of nettle is a fighter for purity, according to Adam, and will take on and battle any impurities that a person is carrying.

Such impurities are regarded by shamans as 'invading spirits' or, in Adam's terminology, 'sins': intrusive energies that can unbalance the mind, emotions, body or soul, and leave us sick, unhappy and 'dis-Graced', feeling alone and unloved by God.

By stroking the patient's body with nettles these energies were engaged by the spirit of the ally-plant which entered the blood (where invading energies congregate) and gave battle to expel them.

The red bumps that appeared on the skin were evidence that these energies were leaving the blood and rising to the surface to avoid the wrath of the nettle-spirit. Once there, they were simply rubbed away and the skin was salved by the use of a cooling and calming herb like chamomile or dock.

Other plants had different affinities and dislikes for certain diseases. For vervain it was depression and disorders of the mind and emotions. Adam taught that vervain can be used as a tonic to help cure depression, paranoia, and insomnia, all of which were again symptoms, as he saw it, of the presence of 'sin'.

Vervain can cure these ailments because its spirit is inclined towards healing these particular aspects of human suffering. Because of this, it could also be used as a charm for protection *from* sin, and to drive away 'evil spirits' before they entered the body at all.

If Adam saw a patient with depression for example, certain healing actions were taken to establish the cause of the illness and if vervain was prescribed, it might be given as a tonic *and* as a charm, with instructions to hang it over the door to the home or to sleep with it beneath the pillow. In this way it removed illness and protected against the circumstances in which it might return.

To work with plants in this way, the healer has to know their spirits intimately, as well as the cause (and not just the symptoms) of the problem the patient is suffering from, and its impact on the soul.

This, then, is the purpose of this book: to introduce you to the soul and the sin eater and Celtic Shaman's ways of working with it, as well as the healing spirit of the plants. Through this, you may become a Reworlder yourself and find your way to Grace.

Jane Gifford is the author of *The Celtic Wisdom of Trees* published in hardback and paperback by Godsfield Press in UK and by Sterling in the USA and Canada under the title *The Wisdom of Trees*. It is also available in German and Japanese.

CHAPTER 1

THE WISDOM OF TREES

Beloved, gaze in thine own heart
The holy tree is growing there;
From joy the holy branches start
And all the trembling flowers they bear.
William Butler Yeats, *The Two Trees*

I once asked Adam what he thought his role was in the world, what healing he had brought, and what his profession had meant to him. "I am a transformer," he replied.

Adam wasn't an arrogant man and his comment wasn't meant to imply that he had special powers or supernatural gifts (to him, the greatest transformers were trees). He meant simply that the job of a sin eater is to transform energy. They take what is bad and replace it with what is good but missing from our souls, so that we can return to *normal*: that state of Grace in which every child is born.

Because of beliefs like this, the orthodox Church has historically had an uneasy relationship with sin eaters, employing them when necessary, spurning them at all other times, and, more usually, regarding them as blasphemers.

The author Bertram Puckle expressed the typical view of the Church in 1926, when he described sin eaters as: "The associates of evil spirits, and given to witchcraft, incantations and unholy practices".[6]

This reaction is largely because sin eating philosophy believes that human beings are born perfect; that having just arrived on Earth from the place of pure spirit, they are untarnished by the world and know nothing of sin.

This may seem an innocent and obvious view to us, but it is still a radical concept to the Church and flies in the face of its teachings which declare that man is born in a state of inherent sin because of the transgressions, long ago, of Eve and the original Adam. To the Church, this sin can only be redeemed through Christ, and anyone else who claims such powers goes against the word of God. If they actually *do* have these powers, it stands to reason, furthermore (Church reason, at least) that they must be consorts of the Devil, for only He is strong or audacious enough to stand against God.

The sin eater's view is closer to common sense. Anyone who has had a child knows that babies are not born 'sinners'; they are innocent of all worldly knowledge and Earthly concepts, and, in any case, expecting a child to come into this world as a Bible scholar is surely asking a lot.

Children are not even born with a capacity *to* sin. As they grow, they are capable of transgressions, of course, against the rules, norms, and mores of the society they live in, but since these rules are ever-shifting by age and by culture, to break them is not to sin, but simply to be alive in a changing world.

Some philosophers, such as Anton LaVey[7] have taken this further (although I cannot say that Adam would necessarily have agreed with them) and suggest that there are some sins which are not transgressions at all, but instinctive parts of human nature which are not only unavoidable, but natural and beneficial, such as the desire for sex and 'the pleasures of the flesh', which is not wrong-doing but our primary motivating force for evolution and progress. Sins like these, they say, have been carefully chosen by the Church to ensure that people will inevitably transgress, as no one can conquer instinct, and nor should they try. Those who feel they have sinned, however, usually have no alternative but to turn to God (and pay the Church) to pray for their forgiveness. The Church is an institution which, therefore stands in the way of human and spiritual progress and keeps us humble and powerless through fear of our damnation.

The next revolutionary concept of sin eaters is that children may be born perfect but they are also born without souls. A newborn child has no moral concepts, but only bodily needs to be satisfied, and a growing and now-incarnate spirit to be nurtured.

With very young children, it is almost as if they are not yet fully 'here', since they are still attached to the spirit-world.

It takes their experience of life and the exercise of their individual wills in the decisions and actions they take for a child to develop a concept of self, of consequences, and of morality. This may take years, but only then can we say that the soul is truly present.

The sin eater's beliefs in this are similar to those of some psychologists such as Lawrence Kohlberg, who studied the development of moral behaviour in children and young adults. Kohlberg's research led him to conclude that children younger than ten do not have a fully developed moral sense (or, in the terms we are using, a soul), but relate to ethical dilemmas in concrete terms and regard rules as fixed and absolute. 'Right' and 'wrong' is based on consequences, not on intentions.

When a young child is told about a boy who broke 15 cups trying to help his mother put them away, and another who broke one cup while he was stealing cookies, the child thinks that the first boy behaved worse. Older children come to understand that rules are not sacred; they are tools we use to get along, and it is our spirits and good or bad intentions which matter, not always what we do. They realise that the boy was trying to help and that even though his actions caused more damage, his intention was good.

There are stages to our moral development, with changes in our understanding taking place throughout. Recently, psychologists have found that our brains continue to grow until the age of around twenty-one, which suggests that our moral development may also continue until this 'coming of age'.

Only then can we say we have 'earned' our souls by challenging ourselves in what Adam called "the field of deeds".

This is sophisticated thinking for people, (sin eaters) who were largely uneducated men living at the edge of communities and practicing a tradition which pre-dated psychology by thousands of years. It demonstrates a more subtle and intelligent understanding of the human condition than that displayed by orthodox religions – as we seen in passages such as this from the Bible: [8]

All that is not of faith is sin
(Romans 14:23)

Behold all souls are mine... the soul that sinneth, the same shall die.
(Ezekiel 18:4)

Or this statement from The Catholic Encyclopaedia: [9]

Sin is nothing else than a morally bad act (St Thomas, "De malo", 7:3), an act not in accord with reason informed by the Divine Law. God... has made us subject to His law, which is known to us by the dictates of conscience, and our acts must conform with these dictates, otherwise we sin.

For those who have a more forgiving and nurturing approach towards the soul, all souls do not belong to God. God is *within us*, and to even be considered as having a soul, the behaviour arising from it must belong to us.

For the sin eater, God *is* the soul, and it and sin are simply forms of energy: the first helping us to evolve towards our destinies so we become all that we have the potential to be, the latter an invasive energy which pulls us away from perfection, but which can be removed so the soul is restored.

This is what Adam meant when he called himself a transformer. Trees, however, were the greatest transformers of all.

Long before James Lovelock arrived at the Gaia principle of life [10] – that our planet is a living and interconnected system, with everything on Earth a part of the whole, the Celts had this same knowledge. To them, rivers and streams were the blood of the Earth and trees were the planet's lungs.

Trees were "the first among plants". Their alchemical powers as the greatest transformers and as guides to the evolving soul were known to the Celts in at least four ways, some practical and some spiritual.

1. TRANSFORMERS OF TOXINS

The Celtic view of trees is now endorsed by science. We know that trees are, indeed, transformers of toxins, and that every tree has the ability to breathe in pollution in the form of the greenhouse gas, carbon dioxide, to purify it through its living alchemy and breathe it back to us as air.

Knowing it is not appreciating it, however, for we have lost our reverence for trees. Ancient civilisations regarded them and their work as sacred in a way we do not. Our lands were once covered in great forests, where people worshipped in groves called *llannerch*, from which the Celtic word *llann* ('church') is derived. In Ireland these groves are called *nemeton*, or *fid-nemed* ('sacred groves of trees'). The great oaks and elms, the yews and the hazel were all Holy, like pillars in some vast cathedral. Through them we could meet a more natural and loving God.

In recent times, we have not only lost our taste for trees but have done our utmost to destroy them. Globally, since the mid-1800s we have overseen the destruction of half of the mature tropical forests that once covered our planet. Almost 800 million hectares of the original 1.6 billion hectares of tropical forest has been destroyed. In the Amazon, the rainforest is being levelled at such an alarming rate that by 2030 80% will be gone and with it, thousands of animal, insect, and plant species will be lost to us forever. In Afghanistan, in the last 20 years, 70% of the country's trees have been felled. In Europe, the devastation of mature deciduous woodland continues.

In Ireland, in 1600, more than 12 per cent of the land was covered by broadleaf forests. By 1800, this had declined to just 2 per cent. In recent years Ireland has been trying to restore its forests but by the year 2000 only 7 per cent of woodlands had been returned (20 per cent of which are in private hands), and the bulk of replanting has been spruce trees rather than native broad leaves.

Human beings have deluded themselves for centuries that we are the 'caretakers' of the planet. Actually we are its nemesis – and our own – since if trees are the lungs of the Earth and we rely on oxygen for our survival, what do we breathe when all the trees are gone and they can no longer transform our pollution?

2. TRANSFORMERS OF HUMAN SPIRIT

Roman authors wrote of Celtic tribes who so venerated trees that they named themselves after them, such as the *Euburones* – 'The Yew Tribe', and the *Lemovices* – 'The People of The Elm'.

Trees were sources of wisdom, and the oak was especially wise. The rustling of its leaves was the voice of the gods, with messages to be interpreted by oracles and seers. Even today, more than 1,600 Irish place names contain the word *doire*: oak wood. These include Derry, or *Doire Cholmcille*, and Kildare or *Cill Dara*: the church of the oaks. Of the 3,000 Holy Wells in Ireland, the majority are marked by a sacred tree.

Irish author Niall Mac Coitir says in *Irish Trees: Myths, Legends & Folklore:*

> With regards to the important place of the sacred tree in Ireland, there is even a special word in the Irish language to describe it, namely a bile. Examples of the bile marking an important place can be found all over Ireland.

Particular trees have their own significance to the Celts.

Hazel is associated with spiritual intelligence. The Well of All Knowledge was surrounded by hazels and the Salmon of Wisdom fed from its fruits.

Yew is the guardian of churches and protector of the dead, and, like the oak, linked to kingship.

Rowan has life-giving properties and is useful to witches and healers.

Elm is a haven for Saints and Holy men.

Birch – the first of the trees according to the ancient ogham alphabet, and known as The Lady of the Woods – stands for purity, grace, love, birth, and new beginnings. Birch is the tree of Arianrhod, the Celtic Otherworld goddess who guards the Silver Wheel of the Heavens and who presides over the initiation of healers and seers.

Each of these trees, and all others, has a particular healing predisposition, which was known to the sin eater and used in herbal cures and tonics for the soul.

All will transform the spirit and simply sitting beneath one will help a troubled mind to let go of cares and lift the weight of the soul, which is why Adam considered them our greatest healers, allies, and teachers.

Each has also lived through generations of human time, seen things we have not, and learned a depth of wisdom we do not yet possess, and so it can guide us towards a bigger picture which puts our cares and troubles into context.

"They are moral guardians," according to Adam, and can help us at all stages in the development of our souls by showing us our place alongside something more eternal than ourselves.

Each tree also has its own personality and resident spirit, and will heal in its own unique way according to the disposition of this spirit. Plant shamans and healers had to get to know these spirits and how to work with them if they were to be effective soul friends and guides to the people who came to them for help.

With this in mind, here are some of the qualities of four of the most important Celtic trees. Since each is associated with a particular element, familiarity with these four alone will provide you with eight healing allies: the trees themselves and the elements they contain, which will be helpful when we look, in chapter three, at methods for healing the soul.

Rowan

The Rowan, or *luis,* gives us the ability to connect with the balancing and regenerative powers of the spirit-world, and is sacred to Brigit, the triple goddess of inspiration, healing, and smithcraft. Its gifts are strength, protection, and the enhancement of psychic and personal power.

In Wales, a cross made from two twigs of rowan tied with red thread was often carried as a charm to protect against evil spirits, or nailed across doorways to prevent unwelcome influences from entering a house. They also ward off ghosts – and were planted on graves so that the dead did not rise from the Earth.

In Ireland, the Shining Ones or Tuatha De Dannan are said to have brought us the rowan tree from *Tir Tairnagire*, the Land of Promise.

By using sticks from the rowan tree, Irish Druids were able to compel the spirits to respond. The rowan is an aid to magic, health, beauty, and longevity, and contains the element of Fire. Rowan is also called The Witch Tree because of the magic contained in its berries, which signal their power by the pentagram at their top, where the fruit is joined to the tree. In *The Story of the Fairy Rowan Tree*: "The woman who is old and who eats a berry from that tree becomes young again, and the maid who is young and who eats a berry gets all the beauty that should be hers of right." [11]

Ash

The Ash, or *nion*, is The Guardian Tree, sacred to the Welsh wizard, Gwydion, and to the Druids, who used it in spells for healing, love, rain-making, prophetic dreams, and prosperity.

It was believed that ash berries placed in the cradle of a newborn will prevent the child from being traded for a changeling by the spirits of the fey, and will also deter serpents (as well as those who act like snakes and try to steal our energy).

Pliny believed that there was such an antipathy between serpents and ash trees that: "If an adder be encompassed round with Ash-tree leaves, she will sooner run through the fire than through the leaves."

Among the Irish, the staff of the chief of the Tuatha De Dannan, the Dagda, is believed to be made of ash wood, and a limestone outline of this staff was found in County Limerick when the Lios, the largest stone circle in Ireland, dating to around 2500 BCE, was excavated.

The Holy Tree of Creevna in Killura was an ash, and was taken in pieces to America by the emigrants who crossed the sea to escape the Great Hunger, since ash stands for good fortune and protects against drowning. The Welsh made the oars of their boats and coracle slates from timber from the ash tree since the wood is impervious to water, and offers protection against the spirit of the waves.

Some say that ash holds the element of Fire, hence its use for Yule logs, where its burning brings the certainty of future prosperity to the family which gathers around it. So many Celtic legends refer to its speed over water and its ability to protect those who sail upon it, however, that it more likely contains the spirit and element of Water.

Certainly, it has watery qualities of healing; its bark is used as a cleanser for the liver and spleen, and its leaves for their diuretic properties.

Yew

Yew (*ywen*) is the Guardian of the Underworld, and brings comfort to the dying with its promise of rebirth and immortality. Ancient yews, some as old as 4,000 years, are planted in churchyards for this reason, and also at the site of springs, which are an entrance to the Underworld.

It is sometimes called 'The Forbidden Tree' because it was used in folk medicine to aid abortions, and so its connection to death continues.

For associated reasons, yew has long been a part of funerary rites, with sprigs thrown into the grave to ensure safe passage to the next life and the soul's transformation beyond death. Its element is Earth.

In recent years, it has been found that taxol, a chemical in the bark, inhibits cell growth and division, and may help to destroy cancer. Its healing power, even in this, is concerned with death.

Beech

Beech (*ffawgddenwas*) is our connection to the gods of wisdom, learning, and the intellect, and is sacred to Ogma, the warrior of the Tuatha De Dannan, who invented the ogham alphabet.

The association of beech with learning is evident in many Celtic languages. The Anglo-Saxon for beech is *boc*, which later became 'book'; the German is *buche*, which became *buch* for book; and the

Swedish word *bok* means both 'book' and "beech tree".

The wood and leaves of the beech can be carried as a charm, and water collected at dawn from the pools in its roots may be drunk to increase creative, intellectual, and divinatory powers. The Bach flower remedy, or a tea made of beech leaf, is good for confidence, relaxation, and for the gentle release of trauma. Its element is Air.

3. TRANSFORMERS OF WORLDS

The talents of trees do not end with their medicinal puirposes for physical ailments, or even their spiritually healing qualities. To the Celts, trees are also the doorways to other worlds.

The most sacred of all is the oak, home to the horned god, Cernunnos, Lord of the Animals, and leader of the Wild Hunt. It is said that the great wizard, Merlin, was sealed in the hollow trunk of an oak and learned his magic from the forest in this way.

There are many other gods and goddesses who inhabit the oak. Nemetona, the goddess of the sacred grove, lends her name to oak sanctuaries. The goddess Brigid, who now lies beneath Croghan Hill in Ireland, once belonged to the Church of the Oak Grove in County Kildare, where a fire was kept burning for her at until 1530, when the sanctuary was Christianised as St Brigit's Cathedral.

The oak, for the Celts, is the *axis mundi*: the cosmic axis, or centre of the world. Its Celtic name, *doir*, is the origin of the word door, with its roots acting as a gateway to the Otherworld, the land of the fey. The guardians of this doorway were the Druids – a title compounded from the Celtic words for "oak" and "wisdom" – for they were 'oak-wise' and had knowledge of other worlds.

The axis mundi or World Tree is a motif that appears in all cultures, and especially those cultures, like the Celts, which are shamanic in their beliefs. It is the point of connection between the sky, earth, and underworld, and provides a means of travel between realms.

It is also the place where the four compass directions meet, and where all of the elements are contained: the branches which dance in the wind and touch the Air, the roots which explore the Earth, and the trunk, which grows powerful through Water (rain) and Fire (sunlight).

To the Norse, the World Tree is *Yggdrasil*, where Odin gained his enlightenment. Within this tree there is a whole cosmos: the tap root forms the shaft of *Mjolnir*, the hammer of Thor, god of thunder, while the *Nidhogg*, a giant serpent beneath the tree at the centre of the Earth, eats the souls of the dead and fights with the eagle that lives in its topmost branches. It is the age-old battle between the primal serpent-soul, the ancient symbol of transformation, and the rational mind or higher self.

In Buddhism, there is a similar myth, but here it is the Bodhi tree which helped Gautama Siddhartha achieve his enlightened state; and there are depictions of world trees in the art and myths of many other cultures, including the Bible, in the form of The Tree of Life and the Tree of Knowledge described in Genesis.

The Celtic World Tree is in Ireland, at Lough Gur in County Limerick, where every seven years the waters recede and the great oak can be seen at the bottom of the enchanted lake. On other days, *Cloch a Bhile* – the Stone of the Tree – stands in a nearby pasture, as a reminder of the tree that supports the world.

There is a rich symbolism in this image of the Irish World Tree. Firstly, that the world of spirit is always there, just below the surface of things, growing in the waters of the soul. This landscape of the unconscious is available to us all whenever we dive these waters or push them aside so we can look more deeply at ourselves.

Secondly, that our lives become richer and we can travel to new horizons when we allow our souls-beneath-the-waters to guide us, when we choose to learn their lessons and become informed by spirit, so we bring soul-energy into our lives as a blessing for the Earth. This is represented here by the Stone of the Tree, which is a metaphor for the spirit world and the soul manifest and made physical.

Making a connection to the World Tree is important for plant spirit shamans and for those who seek healing and inspiration.

One Bardic tradition was for poets to lie beneath oaks and

dream their muse, travelling between worlds so that lyrical wisdom would flow into their veins, like sap from the tree, to feed their visions and fill them with guidance from spirit.

Plant healers would also ask the tree to instruct them in the making of cures or take them to meet with healing spirits so they could find the herbs and treatments needed by their patients. These healers *became* spirit, transformed through the power of the tree, and able to journey to the gods of healing.

4. TRANSFORMERS OF SOUL

There are particular spirits known to shamans whose task it is to escort the souls of the newly-dead into the spirit-world. They are called psychopomps, from the Greek word *psychopompos*, which means 'the guide of souls'.

Among the Welsh, the personification of the psychopomp is Ankou, who collects the souls of the dead and aids them in their passage to the next life. These souls are placed by Ankou on his cart, which is decrepit and broken but continues nevertheless, inexorably and relentlessly, on its languid journey down the dark midnight lanes. According to legend, it is pulled by two horses, one old and thin, the other young and strong, representing the union of opposites and the circle of life.

Ankou is tall and wears a wide-brimmed hat and long black coat made of leaves. Two skeletal companions follow him, tossing the dead into his cart. Some say that he was the first child of Adam and Eve; others that he was the first person ever to die and, because he knows death, he is now its charge.

One story tells how three friends, walking home drunk one night, passed an old man with a rickety cart. Two of them began to shout abuse and throw stones at him, breaking the axle of his cart, which Ankou, silently, with solemn dignity, set about mending. The third friend, wiser and less drunk than the others, recognised Ankou for who he was and helped him repair his cart, replacing the broken axle with a branch of oak, and tying it to the cart with his shoelaces. The next morning, the two friends were dead, their souls collected by Ankou, while the one who had helped was alive, although his hair had turned white and he would never speak of all he had seen.

This legend is a metaphor for what all shamans know: that the tree is the original psychopomp. Ankou, dressed in leaves, driving a cart made of wood, whose axle is repaired by an oaken branch, *is* the tree of souls. When people die, their spirits will instinctively head for a tree or a forest because trees are the doorways through which their souls must pass into the next world.

Sometimes, however, because souls get lost, or if the weight of their sins is too great, they are unable to pass through this doorway and move on. Then it is the job of the sin eater to aid their passage by removing their sin from them and acting as 'midwife to the soul' by standing in for the tree of transformation. This is the role of the psychopomp, and another reason why Adam saw himself as a transformer. The sin eater's role is to become the oak and to act in the way of trees.

THE CELTIC WHEEL OF THE YEAR

The Celtic wheel of the year, or tree calendar [12], such as the one below created by Anna Fraser, provides us with a range of other trees and their connection to the elements, as well as the four directions and the seasons of the year. By spending time with these trees, connecting to their spirits, and doing a little research into the myths surrounding each, it is possible for us to expand our knowledge and develop a healing partnership with different trees and their corresponding elements and seasonal forces, giving us an extensive medicine cabinet of natural healers.

In the tree calendar, the year is divided into 13 months (or 'moons') of 28 days each. The one day remaining to make up the 365 days of the year is the Winter Solstice, the turning point, or centre, of the whole cycle. From this day onwards the days will start to lengthen and a new year will be born. On the Solstice itself, time stops, the doorway between worlds is open, and the spirits walk among us. It is therefore the finest day of the year for magic and for prayer.

"The wheel was conceived by meditating in the woodland and

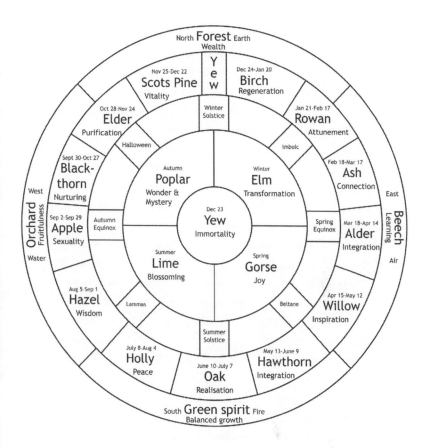

asking the spirits for their guidance," says Anna Fraser. "The answer came almost instantly and made a lot of sense to me as a trained medical herbalist. I was also guided to make a series of tree remedies to go with the wheel of the year, and advised not to make them from picked material (as the Bach remedies and others are), but to 'harvest' the tree essences by swirling water from the legendary *Llyn y Fan Fach* mountain lake (associated with the Welsh legend of the Lady of the Lake who gave us Welsh herbal medicine) around the branches of the living tree.

"Only the Elder tree seemed not very keen to cooperate, but to my shame I ignored this, being enthusiastic to complete the whole series of remedies. When I poured the water from the Elder into a new brown bottle, it spontaneously broke! A great lesson to trust not only the encouraging messages received but also the warnings that something is not quite as it should be.

"The whole thing was quite an important personal milestone for me as it woke me up to the possibility and potential of plant spirit medicine. Up to that time I might have considered the idea only suitable for people with special psychic gifts. But it confirmed the old tradition in virtually all cultures that we gain our knowledge of plant medicine straight from the plants, and via so called 'intuition'.

"Since then, my approach is that plant spirit wisdom is not something you learn via a set of rules; in fact we often need to *unlearn* things, including a whole heap of prejudices we've been lumbered with through the formal education we've received."

By referring to this wheel, and by opening to intuition, you may be inspired to take tree remedies to transform your spirit or even make your own tree remedies if you wish.

Should you desire more love in your life, for example, you might choose to work with the hawthorn, following the procedure Anna suggests.

Asking a Tree for Guidance

Approach the tree and sit with it for a while, letting yourself enter a dreaming space, as the Bards of Wales once did beneath their trees of inspiration.

Then tell the tree what you need from it and ask if it is prepared to work with you in this way.

If the answer is yes, take a few leaves or a twig or two, and thank the tree. Leave an offering for it in return.

If the answer is no, simply move on until you find a hawthorn that will work with you.

When you get home, clean the leaves and twigs and add them to spring or mineral water, then leave them for a few days in sunlight.

Remove the tree material after this and you can then either drink the essence or add it to bath water and bathe in its spirit.

EXPLORATIONS: THE WISDOM OF TREES

The Lord responded
Through words of reconciliation
Conjure noble trees
Taliesin, *Cad Goddeu* – The Battle of the Trees

UNDERSTANDING THE HEALING OF TREES

Shamans have developed a special state of trance consciousness which gives them a connection to the energy or greater spirit of the universe. In the Western world, we call this the shamanic journey.

In essence, it is very simple, and relies more of your ability to relax than to be an expert psychic or master a demanding esoteric technique. It is the approach we will use in this exercise to gain understanding of the wisdom of trees.

Journey into the spirit of the tree

Take a walk out into nature (or you can do this in your own back garden if you have trees you can work with there) and sit down before any tree you feel drawn to. Quietly, in a meditative, focused, and respectful way, simply begin to explore it. Run your hands along its bark, look up and see how it grows, how tall it is, how its branches spread out from the trunk, how its roots seek out the Earth, how its leaves are shaped. Be aware of the elements that form it: the Air, Fire, Water, and Earth that make up its spirit and which feed it and keep it alive. *Notice* the tree and pay attention to what all of this may mean.

Now take your attention *into* the tree and merge with it, as if you were a part of it, the sap rising in its grain, so you feel what it feels and know what it knows, so you sense its qualities and healing intentions. Allow your eyes to go a little out of focus as you look at it so you can *see* the essence beyond its form. When you are ready, lie down among it roots and journey into this essence. Really, this just means closing your eyes and relaxing. Express your *intention* – the purpose for your journey – as well, and keep this in focus as you allow whatever images that come to begin to enter your mind. Intention is the energy that guides shamanic journeys and is best expressed as a positive statement of purpose. On this journey your intention is to meet with the soul of the tree and ask it to teach you its healing powers. So keep this in mind and then relax and receive.

It may be that after a while, pictures begin to form behind your eyelids in response to your statement of purpose, of what the spirit of this tree may look like. Tree spirits often take human form. When this happens, spend some time in conversation with him or her and ask about their healing gifts and how you might work with them to bring greater physical, spiritual, and emotional well-being to your people. Be sure to ask if there is something you can offer in return. Shamans say we must feed our spirits to give them the energy they need to help us. This may take many forms according to what that spirit needs. It could be a ritual, for example, or an offering of some kind. The tree will tell you, so relax and be guided as to what is required. When you are ready to return from your journey, thank the tree for its help and, knowing you can return to its spirit for further guidance at any time, open your eyes and sit up with your back against the trunk. Write down, in a stream of consciousness, all the information you have received, including the ideas and associations that come to you now as you look at or think about this tree.

This, your own experience, is the most important and authentic way to *know* nature: by allowing it to speak to your soul and through your intuition. By doing so, you will know how to work with your ally in ordinary reality too.

TRAVELLING THE SOUL TREE

The World Tree is a gateway to the four directions and can take you anywhere you wish in this world or others. It is also a cauldron for the four elements of Water, Air, Fire, and Earth, and for the powers of the seasons and the wisdom of ages. To know it is to step onto the path of shamanic initiation on your journey to healing.

Although, to the Celts, the oak most symbolised the World Tree, all trees are branches of *the one tree* which spans the entire shamanic universe, not just individual specimens, or representatives of a single species. They are mini World Trees all.

For this next exercise, choose any tree you feel drawn to. Perhaps, as trees, like plants and like all of us, are born of stars and have astrological affinities, you may be more inclined to seek out a tree to which you already have a connection.

Inspired by Claire Nahmad's book of *Garden Spells*, in terms of the zodiacal signs you share in common, these are:

- **Sagittarius:** *Trees:* mulberry, vine, chestnut. *Flowers and herbs:* carnation, sage.
- **Capricorn**: *Trees:* pine, cypress, silver birch, yew, spruce, holly. *Flowers and herbs:* snowdrop, rue.
- **Aquarius:** *Trees:* pine. *Flowers and herbs:* mullein, valerian.
- **Pisces:** *Trees:* pine. *Flowers and herbs:* carnation, violet.
- **Aries:** *Trees:* holly, chestnut. *Flowers and herbs:* thistle, wild rose, gorse.
- **Taurus:** *Trees:* almond, apple, walnut, ash, sycamore, cherry, myrtle. *Flowers and herbs:* lily-of-the-valley, violet, wild rose, coltsfoot.
- **Gemini:** *Trees:* elder, hazel. *Flowers and herbs:* parsley, dill, fern, iris.
- **Cancer:** *Trees:* willow, sycamore. *Flowers and herbs:* poppy, water lily, white rose, honesty.
- **Leo:** *Trees:* palm tree, laurel, pine, oak. *Flowers and herbs:* marigold, sunflower, cowslip, forsythia, hops, peony.
- **Virgo:** *Trees:* hazel, elder. *Flowers and herbs:* rosemary, cornflower, valerian.
- **Libra:** *Trees:* almond, walnut, plum, apple. *Flowers and herbs:* violet, white rose, love-in-a-mist.
- **Scorpio:** *Trees:* blackthorn. *Flowers and herbs:* basil, lesser celandine.

Journey through the doorway

Walk out into nature and find a tree you are drawn to, then lie down next to it so you can journey in the way you now know. In your mind's eye, see that this is a doorway which is open to you, and step through it to explore what waits on the other side.

Intention, as always, is key, so make a statement of purpose before you journey (perhaps to visit the spiritual universe, or to understand the cycle of life and the destiny of souls), then let the spirit of the tree guide you to your answers.

When you are ready to return, retrace your steps, back to the tree and through the doorway it provides, back to your dreaming body, and back to your physical self.

Be sure to close the door behind you by visualising the tree becoming solid once more. Then open your eyes and make a note of all you have learned.

THE ESSENCE OF THE 13 TREES

Thirteen trees were most sacred to the Celts and held all of the healing necessary for the well-being of the people. The poet Robert Graves in *The White Goddess*[13], gives these as:

- *Beth* (Birch)
- *Luis* (Rowan)
- *Nion* (Ash)
- *Fearn* (Alder)
- *Saille* (Willow)
- *Uath* (Hawthorn)
- *Duir* (Oak)
- *Tinne* (Holly)
- *Coll* (Hazel)
- *Muin* (Vine)
- *Gort* (Ivy)
- *Ngetal* (Reed)
- *Ruis* (Elder)

Healers who are inspired by the Celtic Way might get to know all of these trees in turn and prepare remedies from them. Having done so, no other shamanic plant knowledge might even be necessary since these trees are regarded as the greatest healers of all (although there is, of course, no rush to get to know them, and it is better to know one or two well than to have a vague understanding of all).

Journey to the healing essence of the tree

If you wish to explore this form of healing with the essence of the trees, sit with one of them for a while and enter a dreaming space, journeying in the way now familiar to you, into the heart of the tree. Meet its spirit and tell it what you want from it: knowledge of the healing it offers.

Once this guidance is given, say your thanks and goodbyes, and return to normal consciousness, leaving a gift for the tree in return.

Make any notes you wish, so you do not forget, then take a little bark from the tree, or a few leaves and twigs, and go back to your home.

Add what you have gathered to spring or mineral water, and leave it to sit for a few days, then remove the tree material and begin to work with the potion.

Shamans call this *dieting the plant*. It requires that you tune in to your inner state so that you understand how you are feeling physically, emotionally, spiritually, and mentally before you drink any of the tree-water. Then, when you have taken a few sips, sit quietly with the essence and do the same again, noticing any changes that it has brought.

In this way, you learn how the tree spirit works and the healing it offers and, from this, you will begin to understand how it may be used and what it can treat.

CELTIC FEAST TO THE DEPARTED

Apple (*afallen*) is another favourite among healers. In Celtic tradition, it is the tree of prophecy, beauty, and eternal youth, representing the land of the fey, and the place – Avalon: 'the Isle of

Apples' – where King Arthur was taken to be healed.

In the Irish tale of *Connla the Fair*, the land of eternal youth is a magical island where apples keep the people young forever. In the Welsh *Câd Goddeu* (The Battle of the Trees), apple is the noblest tree of all and represents the immortality of the inspired and poetic soul.

Apples are also our connection to the ancestors: the spirits of the dead who have walked the Earth and know its trials and, now that they have passed beyond this, choose to stay with us to offer their wisdom and their love, and to soothe our cares, heartaches, and pains.

As a mark of respect for all that they offer us, in many Celtic homes on Samhain eve October 31 (*Oíche Shamhna* to the Irish, 'the night of the harvest') the ancestors are celebrated and honoured with 'the Dumb Supper', a silent feast for the dead.

A place is set at the head of the table where the ancestors will sit. It is laid with broken crockery, with apples, and with glasses of cider, mead, and apple juice, and not a word is spoken by anyone throughout the meal.

At the end of the feast, the food of the ancestors is taken outside, into the woods, and left before an apple tree at midnight for the spirits of the dead to consume.

Shamans know the power of the ancestors and work with ancestral spirits who whisper guidance into their ears during their healing rituals. They also understand that these spirits must be fed and respected so their healing work can continue.

Journey to the meet the ancestors

To develop an ancestral connection, find yourself an apple tree to dream beneath at midnight (preferably on Samhain eve, when the veil between worlds is thin). Ask silently that the spirit of the tree brings you a vision of the ancestor who will be your guide and help with your healing and that of others.

Once this connection is made, you may return to ordinary consciousness, but before you leave the tree, make an offering to it and the ancestor who stands before it, of whisky, tobacco, and bread.

Walk away without looking back once these gifts are laid and say no word aloud or speak to anyone until you are safe indoors and at home.

CHAPTER 2

THE PLANTS OF GOD

I would conjure shrubs
For I am wanton
With the prophecy of Alchemists.
Taliesin, *Cad Goddeu* – The Battle of the Trees

It is not just trees which are transformers. This is also the healing work of plants, allies with physical and spiritual properties to lead us from ill-health to well-being.

There are many legends describing the origin of healing plants and herbs, all of which explain them as a gift from the land of the fey. In the Welsh tale of *The Physicians of Myddfai*, the story is told of how, many years ago, a farmer from Carmarthenshire, fell in love with the beautiful lady of the lake – the faery, Llyn y Fan Fach – when he took his cattle to graze on the Black Mountains. So deep was his love that, as soon as he set eyes on her, he proposed to marry her, and she consented immediately, but on condition that he would not strike her three senseless blows. He agreed and took her back to the village of Myddfai, where she bore him three sons.

Over the years, however, he did strike her: once a sweet tap in humour for crying at a wedding, once a reproachful nudge for laughing at a funeral, and the third time in play. With this final strike, she disappeared and returned to her mountain home, leaving her husband and sons behind.

In time, the three sons grew to manhood. Llyn y Fan Fach, as good as her word, never saw her husband again, but she continued to meet with her sons and teach them the mysteries of healing herbs. The young men grew wise with this knowledge and became celebrated healers throughout the whole of Wales, where they were known as The Physicians of Myddfai[14], great doctors who passed on the wisdom of the fey and of nearly 200 herbs so that, through them, all people might know how to heal.

Amongst the wise physicians' cures, were these, usually in the form of infusions or poultices, most of which are still in use today:

- **For coughs:** *agrimony*, bruised in a pestle and mortar and the juice strained and mixed with boiled milk.
- **For headaches:** A head-wash of *vervain, betony, chamomile and red fennel*; to be used three times a week.
- **For gastric pains:** *tansy*, mixed with white wine.
- **For nausea:** A pint of *fennel* juice, boiled with a pint of *honey*; a spoonful to be taken first thing in the morning and last thing at night for nine days.
- **For sunburn caught in the fields:** The leaves of *marsh pennywort*, pounded with cream and gently boiled to make an ointment to be rubbed on the skin.

Another traditional tale, this time from Ireland, gives guidance on the attitude of healing and the ways in which plant spirit knowledge should be used.

It tells that long ago, at the waters of a magic well, Brigit came into the world.

From her head there arose a column of fire and, reaching up to it, she took a flame and dropped it on the ground before her, where it became the sacred hearth.

From this hearth she took another flame and swallowed it, and it became the warmth of her heart.

Out of the fire of Brigit's hearth and the waters of her well came all the healing teas. From the fire in her head came poetry, and from the fire in her heart, the warmth of her compassion, which could inflame the world.

Word spread of the gifts of Brigit's fires and people came to learn her healing secrets. The sorrowful ones and the gifted, and all the medicine plants of the Earth gathered there in Brigit's house, and with their leaves, flowers, barks, and roots, and the waters of her well, she taught them to make lotions, salves, and potions for their health.

She gave raspberry leaf to a young woman whose womb needed strength to carry her child, and she was made well. To an old man who could barely walk, she gave black cherry juice, and he was made well. To another with a broken leg, she gave comfrey, and blue cohosh to a woman so her monthly blood would flow without cramps, and all of them were made well. Two men also came, both with terrible leprosy. "Bathe yourself in my well," said Brigit to the first man. He did so and wherever the waters touched, his skin was healed. "Now bathe your friend," she said, but the man backed away and refused in case he became diseased again.

"Then you are not truly healed," said Brigit, and gave him back his leprosy while she healed the second man. "Return to me with compassion," she said. "Then you will be a healer and you also find healing."

From then on Brigit only taught the ways of the plants to those with an open heart.

The spirit of plants, then, is not just for medicinal healing, but compassionate healing, and to become a true healer, and find healing for ourselves in the process, we must become 'plant-like': open, trusting, and willing to turn no one away who comes to us for help.

This message to be like the plants is also be encapsulated in the imagery of the Green Man, one of the best-known of Celtic symbols.

The term 'Green Man' was coined by Lady Raglan in 1939, in her article *The Green Man in Church Architecture*, published in *The Folklore Journal*. It refers to a figure (sometimes also known as Jack-in-the-Green or John Barleycorn) found in sculptures or carvings in churches and other places of power with a pre-Christian history.

Green Men are male human faces (their somewhat female equivalents are Sheela na Gig) surrounded by leaves and vines sprouting from their nose, mouth, and hair, which may bear flowers or fruit.

These foliate heads show plants taking human form, or humans becoming plant-like. Probably they derive from, and represent the

Celtic nature gods, Cernunnos and Viridios, and are most likely symbols of power, fertility, rebirth, and oneness with the Earth, reminding us of the need to adopt these qualities in ourselves if we wish to be great healers.

HOW PLANTS HEAL

Like the Celtic trees, plants have a predisposition to help and to heal in particular ways, which are known, simply, by asking them what these might be, or by observing them, tuning in to them, and exploring their qualities so their message is heard and their attributes known.

This concept – that plants themselves will tell us what they are used for – is an ancient one, known to the shamans of all traditions, who recognise the spiritual powers and qualities of plants by their colours, perfumes, the places and ways in which they grow, and the moods they evoke in us when we interact with them.

Some plants are now so synonymous with a mood or feeling, in fact, that we have an automatic response to them. When a lover gives us roses, we may admire the beauty and perfume of the flowers, but it is *love* that we feel. The medium *is* the message.

The 16th century alchemist and philosopher, Paracelsus, was among the first to recognise this and to describe the personality of plants and their ability to communicate their healing purpose, in his treatise on the *Doctrine of Signatures*.

This proposes that 'the finger of God', or the creative energy of the universe, has placed a seal on plants to tell us their medicinal uses. Their appearance is the means by which they communicate these uses and is 'the light of nature'.

Paracelsus noticed that the qualities of plants were reflected in the way that they looked and the qualities they contained: that the willow tree grows in damp places, for example, and will heal conditions such as rheumatism, which are caused by a build-up of fluid on the joints; that the garlic stalk resembles the windpipe and can, in fact, be used to treat throat and bronchial problems; that spleenwort would treat ailments of the spleen because the sori on the backs of its fronds look like the organ it is named for; that liverwort, which resembles the liver in outline, would cure the problems of this organ; and that toothwort would help with dental pain because the flowering part looks like rows of teeth. As strange as it may seem, many of these cures have been shown by science to work.

Underlying Paracelsus' realisations was the understanding that nature is a living organism and an expression of 'the One Life', meaning that man, plants, and all things in the universe, share the same essence. Because of this, the inner nature of plants can be read from their outer forms or signatures and we respond to them in terms of the qualities we share in common.

The poet and writer, Ralph Waldo Emerson, said much the same thing in his essay on *Nature*:

Every appearance in nature corresponds to some state of mind, and that state of the mind can only be described by presenting that natural appearance as its picture. An enraged man is a lion, a cunning man is a fox, a firm man is a rock, a learned man is a torch. A lamb is innocence, a snake is subtle spite; flowers express to us the delicate affections. Light and darkness are our familiar expression for knowledge and ignorance; and heat for love. Visible distance behind and before us, is respectively our image of memory and hope. [15]

Terence McKenna, the 20th century philosopher and ethnobotanist, said something similar: "Nature is alive and talking to us. This is not a metaphor."

The appearance of a plant, therefore, *is* the gateway to its soul and to our own. Paracelsus called this 'the Spirit of Life'.

One example of a plant that can be known from its signature is snakeroot, also called seneca root, or senega. Its tap root, brown on the outside, pale yellow inside, grows in a spiral which looks like a snake and, because of this, it is used – in many cases, effectively – as a cure for snake bites within a number of healing traditions, including those of the Senega tribe of America, after whom it is named.

That is not its only use. It will also work on 'snake-like' parts of the human body, such as the spinal column, nerves, and circulatory system, to treat the ailments and conditions which occur there.

The spiritualist, Edgar Cayce, referred to snakeroot in his channelled spirit messages, and recommended it as a cure for neuropathic conditions (chronic pain as a result of injury to the nervous system), its actions being to make "adjustments to the whole spinal column" and bring the nerve centres "to their normal condition".

His recipe for this was:

Snakeroot: 2 ounces
Yellow Dock root: 2 ounces
Burdock root: 2 ounces
Dog Wood bark: 2 ounces
Prickly Ash bark: 2 ounces, and
Elderflower: 4 ounces

The ingredients are added to a gallon of distilled water and reduced by simmering it down to a quart. It is then strained and four ounces of grain alcohol are introduced, along with three drams (about 9ml or three teaspoons) of Balsam of Tolu. A teaspoonful is taken after every meal and before bed.

Another of his recipes was for the intestines (also snake-like), and acted as a stimulant for the pancreas and liver, and to bring "balance in the stomach itself, and to perform the correct intestinal digestion throughout the system". To one gallon of rain water are added:

Snakeroot: 2 ounces
Wild Cherry bark: 4 ounces
Yellow Dock root: 2 ounces
Burdock Root: 2 ounces, and
Elderflower: 2 ounces

This mixture is reduced by slow boiling, then strained and added to four ounces of alcohol and three drams of Balsam of Tolu. A teaspoon is taken four times a day, combined with a twice-daily massage with very cold water from the first cervical to the sacrum, which should then be "rubbed with a rough coarse towel".

More spiritual uses included protection from 'snakes in the grass' (in other words, those who wish to stab you in the back, take what is yours, or are envious of what you have). In one recipe, a piece of the root is added to cologne and used as a perfume to bring good fortune and protect the wearer from snakes among friends and acquaintances. In another, a little powdered snakeroot is worn in the shoes to protect against actual snakes and to ensure that evil magic is not absorbed when you are among unworthy people.

The Doctrine of Signatures may sound a little far-fetched to consumers of modern science with its emphasis on lab tests, data and evidence, but, strangely enough, scientists themselves don't find it that odd.

According to a piece published on the BBC News website on tribal cures for modern ailments:

Pharmaceutical companies are returning to the Earth's forests in their search for new medicines to cure some of mankind's biggest killers, such as Aids, cancer, and malaria. This is called bioprospecting. But randomly collecting plants is not the most effective way to do this.

According to Conservation International (CI), an American environmental organisation, if plant collectors work alongside the tribe's shaman, or medicine man, they are 50% more likely to find an active compound.

They say that over 74% of today's plant-derived medicines were previously used for similar purposes by indigenous people. On the organisation's first bioprospecting trip with the Trio shaman Amasina, they found two plant species new to western science, and 14 other plants with previously unknown medicinal properties. [16]

At the root of these new scientific discoveries is traditional plant spirit shamanism, which works by the medicine man tuning in to the spirit of the plant and asking what it is used for and how best to work with it. Inevitably, *The Doctrine of Signatures* plays a part in this and is the means by which shamans identify the plant in the first place or have their attention drawn to it.

Thus, even people who put their faith in science and deride traditional cultures and their 'primitive' medicine, are, for all their pill-pushing and popping, ultimately backdoor consumers of plant spirit wisdom and shamanic knowledge.

Scientists at Kew Gardens in London are also working with the wisdom of traditional healers in a new project to explore the world of healing plants. According to an article on the ancient secrets of plants' miracle cures in *The Observer* newspaper:

> Both the old and new understanding of the UK's wild flowers and herbs are being brought together in a remarkable scientific programme [where] our ancient knowledge of the healing properties of plants, contained in remedies written down by herbalists over the centuries, is being given new relevance by the ability of molecular technology to unlock their secrets.

The search for medicines from plants is nothing new. For years pharmaceutical investigators have searched forests and swamps around the world looking for a cure for cancer or heart disease. Aspirin came from the willow tree, and the cancer drug taxol was found in the Pacific yew tree. But the search is now being conducted among the 1,600 species of plants native to the UK. At Kew's Jodrell laboratory, scientists carry out molecular tests, looking for the active compounds in different plants to see whether there is any kind of scientific basis for the claims made by herbalists about particular plants. One of the first to show promise is figwort, a dark-leaved plant found in Northern Ireland and Norfolk, where it grows in shady woods and meadows. [17]

Figwort grows in damp, deciduous, woodland, and has heart-shaped, reddish-brown or purple flowers about one centimetre long, which look bruised or inflamed since the rest of the plant and the flowers below this eruption of red are greenish-yellow. Following *The Doctrine of Signatures*, it should come as no surprise that figwort has been used for centuries to treat problems such as eczema, psoriasis, ulcers, itching, and irritation, all of which usually lead to red, inflamed, areas of the skin. It is also a heart stimulant, as the shape of the flowers and their blood-red colour suggest.

The apothecary, Nicholas Culpeper described in his enduring guidebook *Culpeper's Herbal*, published in 1628, how a "decoction of the herb, taken inwardly, and the bruised herb applied outwardly, dissolves clotted and congealed blood within the body", and an infusion of the whole plant will also dry up ulcers.

Nearly 500 years later, Professor Monique Simmonds, the chief plant scientist at Kew, commented that:

We think that [figwort] might be particularly promising for diabetes. Many of these patients suffer from leg ulcers, and sadly these sometimes result in an amputation because there is not that much which works by way of treatment.

The scientists at Kew, quoting directly from *The Doctrine of Signatures*, also pointed out to the *Observer* newspaper:

The names of plants often give away their uses. The herb lovage, for example, won its name because of its reputation as an aphrodisiac. Sage is a herb that has been connected with wisdom down the ages, and now for the first time we can see whether it really helps with cognitive ability or memory, said Simmonds.

Around the world, it is used by many communities to help the memory. Researchers at King's College London and Newcastle University have worked with Kew to identify that it does affect receptors in the brain, and work is still continuing into exactly what it does. One discovery was that people taking sage oil extract showed a marked improvement in their memory.

Figwort Infusion

To make an infusion of figwort, pour a cup of boiling water onto 1-3 teaspoonfuls of the dried leaves and let it stand for fifteen minutes.

It can be drunk three times a day, but if you have a known or suspected heart condition, this would be better done under the guidance of a medical herbalist or other qualified health practitioner. [18]

RESPECT AND ADMIRATION FOR THE PLANTS

To be an effective plant spirit shaman, it is not enough, however, to simply identify a plant from its signature. Shamans know that respect for the plant, a proper attitude, and adherence to ritual procedures are also important when working with these healing spirits.

Adam always asked permission of a plant before picking it and left a gift in exchange for a few of its leaves or flowers, just as you have done in your work so far with trees. When dealing with the most powerful teacher plants he was also careful to purify himself through ritual bathing and a period of fasting before he even entered the field to collect the plant. It is also common for plant healers to chant, sing, or offer invocations and prayers to the herbs they collect before they pick them, as a mark of respect, and to form a healing bond with their spirits.

The *Carmina Gadelica* is a volume of charms, hymns, and invocations from the Highlands and islands of Scotland, collected in the 1800s by Alexander Carmichael [19]. It contains several prayers like this to particular plants, including club moss, ragwort, primrose, juniper, and shamrock. This one for 'The Gracious Root':

I will cull my gracious root
As Brigit culled it with her one hand
To put essence in breast and gland of milk
To put substance in udder and in kidney
Butter and curd, fat and cheese
Like stream pouring from breast of fortune

Like honey distilling from the love on high

Thou only anointed white One of the God of grace
Keep Thou for me mine own
Keep Thou to me the share of grace
Keep Thou from me the goods of foes
Keep Thou from me the folk of lies
Keep Thou from me the [visiting] of death
Keep Thou from me the visiting of harm
Keep Thou from me the re-pairing
Keep Thou from me the stillborn calf…

The plant of substance be mine.

There are various stories in Celtic literature which warn of the need for such precautions because, like all of us, plant spirits do not react well to being taken for granted or having their powers abused. It is said that mandrake, for example, if simply pulled from the ground, will emit a scream so potent and terrifying that it is enough to kill a man or send him mad.

In other examples, like the story below, of Jack Fox and the Leprechaun [20], plant spirits and the entities who guard them may not respond so aggressively but, still, if our intentions and approach are not pure, we will get little from them except broken dreams and wasted time.

Dandelions are some of the most useful plants. To find out how long you will live, blow once on the seeds and count those that are left. This, in years, is the age you will live to. They are great healers too, especially of bladder and liver, and, with the blessings of Brigit, they may be used for divination. It is also said that, in fields of dandelions, the pot of gold can be found at the end of the rainbow.

Dandelions are guarded, however, by leprechauns, and if our intention in gathering them is not deemed correct, we can be sure of tricks being played on us by the guardians of dandelion gold. Such was the case with Jack Fox.

Every *Imbolc* (February 1), hundreds of people visit *Tobar Muire* (Mary's Well), near Dundalk, where they crawl on their hands and knees nine times around the well, in a Westerly direction, as this will cure all ailments.

Jack had just completed this ritual and was heading back to his fields, his scythe upon his back, when, from the hedgerows, he heard a sound like that of a cricket. The hairs on his neck stood up as he realised what it was. Pushing the bushes aside, sure enough, he came upon a leprechaun.

Jack remembered that the little people could show you the way to the pots of gold at rainbow's end, but only if it was needed for the healing of others. Jack laid down his scythe and crept closer.

"Bail ó Dhía ar an obair," said Jack: "God bless the work."

"Go raibh maith agat," said the leprechaun: "Thank you and bless you too."

"What is your name?" asked Jack.

"Night and Day and Far Away," the leprechaun answered.

"That is a strange name."

"And so is yours, Jack Fox."

"How do you know my name?" asked Jack.

"Why wouldn't I? I have been living on your farm for longer than you have!"

"Well, then, if you have been living on my land," said Jack, "it is time you paid your rent. Take me to the end of the rainbow where your pot of money lies, for I know people who need the gold and the healing it might bring them."

The leprechaun laughed and tried to dismiss the stories of gold as nonsense, but Jack would have none of it. "Take me to your gold or I will roast you over a griddle!" he demanded.

The little man looked frightened. "All right then, I'll tell you where it is," he said. "Come on and follow me."

They crossed meadows, stiles, and streams, before they came to a field of a million dandelions. "There," said the leprechaun, pointing to one particular flower, "The gold is beneath that *caisearbhán*. Dig there. And now I must be on my way."

"Swear that the gold is there," said Jack, "and then I will let you go."

"I swear on all my ancestors."

"All right, then", said Jack, "Away you go and *slán!*"

"*Slán is beannach*: Health and blessing," said the leprechaun, and away he went.

Jack had no spade with him and so, to mark the place of the gold, he took off his sock and put it over the dandelion. Then he went home to fetch his tools.

"I have found the leprechaun's gold!" he shouted to his wife. "We will be rich and never have to work again!" He whistled with delight as he grabbed his spade and returned to the field of dandelions.

But when he got there, on every dandelion in the whole fifty acres there was a sock exactly the same as his own.

"The leprechaun has fooled me!" he bellowed. "I could dig for a thousand years and never find the place." Angry and downcast, he threw down his tools and went home to tell his wife of the disaster.

"You forgot the truth of the matter, Jack Fox," was all his wife had to say. "Plants and gold are there for the good of others, not to feed a man's greed. Still and all, at least I won't have to knit you another sock for as long as I live!"

And with that they burst out laughing at the humour of the lesson.

This need to respect the plants and their healing gifts is also alluded to in the myth of the salmon of knowledge:

The salmon, oldest and wisest of creatures, swam in the Pool of Wisdom in a grove of hazel trees, into which the nuts of the wise tree fell.

The Druid, Finegas, watched over the tree and the salmon for seven years, until the time was right for him to eat the fish and to receive from it all knowledge.

As the salmon roasted, however, Finegas, believing his work to be done, left his pupil, Demme, in charge, who, in turning the fish, was burned when some of its oil spat onto his thumb. Without thinking, he put it into his mouth to soothe the burn and, in that moment, he received the wisdom it contained.

Finegas, despite his seven-year vigil, was left with nothing, while Demme went on to become a great and wise leader, later joining the warriors of the Fianna as the greatest hero of all: Fionn Mac Cumhal.

And the moral of this tale? Well, one moral, at least, may be that, no matter how dedicated we are in our guardianship, protection, and respect for the plants and the animals that feed from them, and to the ecosystem of which we are a part, our dedication must be continuous and constant, for the single occasion when we abandon our duty could be the very time we lose our connection to the magic we most need.

We should also realise the true gravity of our actions when we pick and use plants. As Adam once remarked, whenever a plant is used to heal ourselves or others, something dies. Most likely we are killing the plant to cure the patient.

There is always a sacrifice in nature. It is only the arrogance of our species which would convince us that plant life is less precious than human life. We should keep in mind exactly what the plant is giving us – its life and its very soul (the energy it contains) – when we pick it and use it in our medicines.

Although Adam lived in a small village on the borders of Wales and had little contact with other healers, I have heard the same words repeated many times by plant spirit shamans in several different countries of the world. Most of them were simple men and women who had become skilled in their practice by working with plants in the fields. They had not received their wisdom from books, the internet, or from email correspondence with other healers.

When I asked how they knew about the need to respect plants, or why it was that, in most parts of the world, they practiced the same healing methods, whether a Shipibo shaman in South America or a sin eater in Wales, without once communicating with each other, all of them replied: "Our spirits told us."

Sometimes they meant by this the spirits of the plants, or their guides, ancestors, and tutelary spirits; sometimes they meant that the information came from their own spirits or souls (or maybe they are one and the same, since the same spirit flows though us all). But, always, just being with the plant will provide the answer.

Alfred Vogel, the Swiss naturopath and European nature doctor, expressed similar views to these medicine men and their commitment to respect for the plant:

> Nature gives us everything we need for the protection and maintenance of our health. [But] if we want to achieve something, we must abide by Nature and its rules.

According to the medicine men I have met, plants are aspects of God, just as we are, and respond, as we do, to love.

Their cures arise because they provide us with a doorway to love – their energy and that of the wider universe allowing us to tap into the greatest source of power for our emotional and physical well-being. But love must be handled carefully.

The prescriptions, taboos, and precautions surrounding plants are present to protect healers and their patients as much as they are the plants.

Some of the ways in which this respect is demonstrated include offerings to Nature.

Adam left gifts for the plants he worked with in exchange for their leaves and berries; usually a little tobacco, a drop of whisky or mead, or perhaps a few coins, but sometimes they were more unusual. He swore, for example, that one plant preferred cheese. No matter how strange, he went along with these requests from the spirit of the plant, on the non-judgemental assumption that it knew its own mind, and its likes and dislikes, better than he did.

In the West, we gain most of our knowledge about plants from science books taught to us in uninspiring lessons in the classrooms of city schools, so we are not used to nature as a living and intelligent force. In this context, offering cheese to a plant seems anything but normal, but such gifts are frequent and common in other cultures.

In the Andes of Peru, for example, an *offerenda* is simply an acknowledgement of the obvious: that there is a unity between man and nature and each species must respect the other. It is also a recognition of the fact that we cannot just take from nature without giving back.

An *offerenda* is normally a piece of paper (about 12 inches or 30 cm square), onto which gifts that the spirits enjoy, such as candies, corn, peanuts, herbs, shells, flowers, and coins, are placed in formal arrangement, before the paper is ritually folded and tied with wool or string.

The ceremony takes place in nature, usually at a high spot, such as the top of a mountain. Prayers and requests, or more likely, expressions of gratitude, in the awareness that all that you ask for is already yours; you simply have to claim it, are then made, and the package is given to a fire made just for this purpose.

In Haiti, the ritual is even simpler, and in some ways reminiscent of the sin eater's practices. Here, when the *medsen fey* (the 'leaf doctor' or shamanic herbalist) picks his leaves, payment is left for the spirits, in the form of tobacco, rum, or a few coins.

One *medsen fey* described the practice in words which suggest the reverence in which nature is held:

I must pay the spirit for the help it gives me. At every crossroads on my way to gather leaves, I sing and bury coins in the earth. The value is irrelevant, it is respect that is important

When I reach the plant I want, I sing to it and tell it of the task that lies ahead, asking for its help. Once it has given permission and the leaves are gathered, they must never touch the earth because that would be an insult.

It is good practice, and necessary if we want to gain the support of the plant and avoid the tricks of spirit, to show similar respect when we gather leaves or work with our plant spirit allies.

Always leave something in return for what you take, and maintain an attitude of respect, admiration – even awe – for the spirit of the plant, its courage in offering itself to you, and the sacrifice it is making.

Rituals of Purity

Another way in which respect is shown is through the practices of ritual purity that are observed before plants are gathered or worked with, and the taboos that often surround the shaman's intake of food, drink, and sex.

Adam would fast, bathe himself in floral waters, avoid alcohol, and remain quiet and contemplative, shunning the company of others before his forays into nature. Similar practices are followed in most shamanic cultures of the world, such as in the jungles of the Amazon, where this almost-identical procedure is known as the shaman's diet.

The shaman's diet involves prescribed actions and non-actions which are restrictions on the behaviour of the shaman so he is in the proper frame of mind for his encounter with the plants.

It may include the learning of magical songs called *icaros* to call and make contact with the spirits and invoke the power of the plant, and always it involves wider dietary requirements which allow the transmission of healing and knowledge. These prohibit foods such as pork, fats, salt, spices, condiments, and alcohol, leaving the shaman with a healthy but very bland menu so he is not overwhelmed or confused by flavour and fragrance, but can more easily sense the attributes of the plant he is working with.

The blandness of the diet also serves to weaken his emotional attachments to everyday life and the habits it involves, many of which come from, or are associated with, food and its various rituals. For the same reason, he will follow a prohibition on sexual activity, since sex is another distraction which may inhibit spiritual potential by focussing attention on the body.

Detachment, reflection, and removal from the physical world, are the pre-requisites for shamans who are learning the ways of a particular plant. They may spend weeks or months in purification and retreat to release their hold on everyday life and quiesse the rational mind so their spirits can expand into nature, just as Adam did in his fasting.

The shaman's intention in this remains key. In following the diet, to whatever level and nuance, as with so much of plant work, his purpose is a rigorous desire to meet with the spirits of the plants in an attitude of utmost respect, not just to ingest them for their physical properties. This means taking them with courage and with full awareness of what they truly represent: doorways to a whole and other intelligence.

Understanding That All Plants Are Precious

When I first met Adam and saw his garden, I was surprised that it appeared so unkempt and that weeds had taken over and were growing, in some strange order, right alongside desirable garden plants such as roses and useful herbs.

As I got to know him, however, I began to see the logic: that it is the Western mind which judges and orders plants according to an arbitrary decision about what is 'beautiful' and what is not. As I learned more from him, I came to truly appreciate nettles (one of Adam's favourite plants, but the very ones that I, and many other people have struggled to get rid of in our own gardens). While unloved by gardeners, nettles are some of our most powerful allies in their ability to cure disease and fortify the spirit.

Through my friendship with Adam, I realised that there is power and beauty in all plants – and in all parts of a plant – so nothing need ever be wasted. We can learn from each petal, root, leaf, or fragment of bark, and it is not just the accepted, 'pretty', or obvious plants that we should seek out and work with.

Those that we choose (or which choose us) could call to us for many different reasons, not just their presence in a seed catalogue or a garden centre. Their colours or scents might be significant, triggering memories of well-being or suffering, in either case telling us something beyond their forms of importance to our souls. The way that they grow, their names, or what they represent might also have meaning for us.

This, of course, is *The Doctrine of Signatures* again, but it is also more than that. The process of selecting a plant to work with or to diet *should* be intuitive and emotional, not rational and conscious, because there is a respectful honesty in this too, where we meet our allies heart-to-heart, soul-to-soul, and with our full attention and willingness to connect.

There is a beauty in all plants and they will sing to our souls if we let them, irrespective of their 'status' in the world. Recognising, appreciating, and honouring that beauty is also a mark of respect.

HERBS OF SUN AND MOON

Like humans, all plants came from the stars, and each has an affinity with a particular planet. Plant powers are enhanced by planting, harvesting, and preparing them under the influence of their planetary connection. This is another form of respect for the plant by the shaman who wishes to work with it, since he meets it on its own terms.

The two greatest influences on any plant are the sun and moon. Some plants are solar, 'masculine', 'bright', 'fiery', filled with passion and vigour, and most powerful during daylight. Others are lunar, 'feminine', 'softer', 'watery', perhaps they release their scent after nightfall, and exude a gentler energy that is more pronounced under moonlight.

It makes sense that each type should be gathered and prepared at the time when it is most full of power – lunar herbs at night, solar powered herbs by day – and that the shaman feels a connection to the planet as well as the plant that he is working with.

Lunar Herbs

Shamans say that the moon is made of water. While it rules all plant growth and every herb has at least a little lunar energy, the moon has a more potent effect on herbs which have to do with the emotional qualities or watery functions of the body, such as fertility, sexuality, sleep, dreams, and memory, as well as bodily fluids, like blood, sweat, tears, lymph, saliva, and urine.

One way for the shaman to honour this and to develop his own affinity for water is to bathe and cleanse himself before gathering or using these herbs. Another is to keep his movements 'fluid' while gathering, so that he blends with nature itself.

Our bodies and our planet are comprised of two-thirds water,* and most of it is in constant flow. At the human and planetary level, the processes of circulation, secretion, precipitation, and evaporation are important for health, and there are herbs that promote the balance of these fluids in the body; some demulcent and some astringent.

Following *The Doctrine of Signatures*, herbs that aid the circulation tend to be salty and moist, like body fluids themselves, and include Irish moss, comfrey, and marshmallow.

Those which strengthen the reproductive system tend to look like the sexual organs. Hence, the leaves of wild yam (which can be used by menopausal women instead of oestrogen-based hormone replacement therapies) are shaped like the womb, while black cohosh (used to treat infertility) has a long, phallus-like flower.

Plants which increase male sexual potency also resemble or suggest the sexual organs – like pumpkin seeds or saw palmetto. The latter, like the testes or prostate in shape, have been found, in a study of 1,098 men with prostate problems, to be an aid to better sexual health. Researchers compared saw palmetto with a commercial pharmaceutical treatment and found that both were equally effective after six months, although the herb caused fewer side-effects (and, of course, it is plentiful and free).

Sleep and dreams are also affected by the moon, and lunar herbs have the power to induce restful sleep and peaceful or prophetic dreams. They include willow bark and wild lettuce, which are sedative and analgesic.

Those which aid memory (and often the flowering of intuition

---

* In actual fact, our water levels vary throughout life. As fetuses, we are 99% water. As adults, we are 70% water. And, if we are lucky enough to live to old age, we will end our days as 50% water.

and the higher senses) include sage, gotu kola, and lotus seeds, which will also help an anxious mind to relax.

Perhaps the greatest gift of the lunar herbs, however, is their ability, through the cooling power of Water, to reduce 'heat' in the body, whether this is literal and physical, or mental and emotional giving rise to inflamed passions like jealousy, rage, anger and some forms of addiction.

In the body, these herbs absorb toxins and help us to expel them. For the mind and emotions they are calming. Mostly, they are bitter, like horseradish, endive, and dandelion, or moist, like cucumber and chickweed. The latter, made into an ointment, will relieve inflammations like eczema and psoriasis by pulling dryness out of the body, while other moon herbs are so powerful, it is said, that they can even draw out cancers. These include violet, fleur-de-lys, blue flag, and pumpkin seeds (for cancer of the prostate).

Solar Herbs

The solar herbs, following Paracelsus, are recognised by their bright appearance and 'fiery' or luminous qualities. Many, such as chamomile, St John's Wort, marigolds, and, of course, sunflowers, have gold or yellow flowers which bloom around the time of the Summer Solstice. Sunflowers even follow the path of the sun, facing east as it rises and bending to the west as it sets. For the Celts, the sun was the great preserver of life, and the herbs associated with it tend also to stimulate vitality, life, light, energy, and brightness, bringing balance to those who are suffering from a deficiency (or excess) of libido and engagement with the world. They restore equilibrium to the physical system, provide a tonic for the heart and emotions, and promote the flow of good energy.

Angelica is one such herb, which will reduce the effect of fevers and inflammations by consuming them with its own heat. Chamomile and celandine also reduce fire in the body, while juniper soothes inflammations and brings rejuvenating warmth to rheumatic conditions, which may be caused by dampness and cold.

Many solar herbs are adaptable like this, and will relieve cold symptoms (whether of body or emotions such as a 'cold heart') by lifting the spirits and bringing their sun-like qualities to bear on mucus membranes and congested lungs, while cooling us down and absorbing excess physical or emotional heat.

The greatest herb of the Celts was mistletoe, which, growing on the sacred oak, and white-gold in colour, was considered *the* plant of the sun. During the winter it resembled the pale misty sun and brought the promise of summer's return. It was ceremonially harvested on the Solstice and used for a number of medical and magical purposes, including protection from fire and lightning.

Sprigs of mistletoe were also hung in stables to protect livestock from the magic and mischief of faeries, and over cradles to protect sleeping babies from witches. As long as a sprig remained in the home, love would never leave, and this is the origin of the English custom of kissing beneath the mistletoe at Yuletide. A sprig placed beneath a young woman's pillow will also bring dreams of a future husband.

Another Celtic sun herb is St John's Wort. The birthday of the Saint the plant is named after is said to be six months before the birth of Christ, or June 24 according to the Roman calendar: midsummer's day, when the sun is at its highest. St John's Wort has golden flowers which radiate like the rays of the sun and appear around the time of the Solstice. In mediaeval days it was therfore known as s*ol terrestris*, 'terrestrial sun'. Once it has flowered, its leaves become mottled with red and, with its flowers gone, the plant looks 'beheaded'. This reflects the fate of its patron, who was killed at the request of the dancer, Salome.

St John's Wort – and all solar plants – are bright like the sun and able to counteract the forces of darkness and depression. Thus, according to Richard Folkard, writing on plant lore and legends in 1884, St John's Wort is "a preservative against evil spirits, phantoms, spectres, storms, and thunder" [23]. It protects against negativity or bad spirits, and can be hung over doorways to guard those inside from malevolent energies. Indeed, its generic name, *Hypericum*, from the Greek, means 'power over apparitions'.

Contemporary research confirms that the oil in St John's Wort has powerful anti-bacterial and anti-viral actions, which, invisible to the eye, would be considered in medieval times to be phantoms and spectres. Hence, the work of St John's Wort is, indeed, to preserve the soul.

GATHERING AND DRYING HERBS
In gathering herbs, there are certain practical guidelines to be followed beyond the ritual ones, since the levels of their active ingredients are higher at the end of their periods of greatest growth. For maximum effectiveness, plants should be gathered as follows.

- Barks and roots in spring, prior to the aerial plant development
- Leaves before the plant flowers
- Flowers on the first day of opening
- Roots may also be gathered in the autumn, after the flowering season ends.

Lunar herbs are best gathered at night, under the light of the moon. A full moon is best because of its 'drawing' actions on the fluids in the plants, which will cause them to swell with power. Solar herbs are best picked during the day, in the cool of the morning, as too much heat from the sun will dry out the oils in their leaves.

Only the healthiest and greenest leaves should be picked, with any that are imperfect left on the plant, along with those closest to the root. It is also important to gather in an area free from chemical and industrial pollution, at least a quarter of a mile from roads.

Leaves, stems, and flowers can all be dried by spreading them in single layers on a flat surface, allowing the air to circulate around them, and in either sunlight or shade, depending on their solar or lunar natures. Lunar drying takes longer but preserves more of the herb's aroma.

Roots are the most difficult to dry, and it is usually best to cut the stems of larger ones, such as liquorice and burdock, after they have been washed, and then tie and hang them until they become brittle.

Dried herbs should be kept out of direct sunlight, and are best stored in dark glass jars or bottles with tight fitting lids, as other containers, such as cardboard boxes or fabric bags, will absorb the oils from the plants.

SINNER'S HERBS

David Hoffmann, in *Welsh Herbal Medicine,* writes that:

Druidic medical therapeutics is an interesting combination of mystical and herbally rational techniques... The Druids devoted considerable effort to study the medicinal properties of plants, believing some herbs to be endowed with magical virtues.

This was certainly Adam's stance. His belief was that illness arose as a result of sin: an energy that gathers in us through our exposure to unwholesome conditions or circumstances. This energy acts like a virus, growing and consuming our health and natural energies and sapping us of strength.

Thus, all illnesses have a spiritual cause which can only be cured by spiritual intervention. This is the job of the plants, which have the dual effect of treating the physical or other symptoms and, at the same time, curing the malaise of the soul.

Illness can therefore also be prevented by ensuring that the energies of the body are balanced, whole, flowing correctly, and strong enough to resist external influences. Herbs are available for this too.

These 'sinner's herbs' provide a daily tonic, which may be drunk as a simple tea by adding a few of their leaves to hot water, with honey to taste, and allowing the brew to infuse for a few minutes.

Nettles: The first and foremost among these are nettles. The stinging structure of a nettle is similar to a hypodermic needle and enables the spirit of the plant to be 'injected' into the system, thereby facilitating its healing. If you'd rather not be stung, however, the tea is refreshing and tasty, and a good source of iron, calcium, and folic acid, providing you with a general tonic which will fortify your body. It is also a blood purifier and can help in the treatment of anaemia, excessive menstruation, rheumatism, hay fever, and skin complaints such as eczema.

Nettle leaves can also be placed in a muslin bag which is added to a hot bath. Bathing in this allows the nettle spirit to more gently enter the body so its work of purification can take place, while the bag protects the bather from stings.

Vervain: Also known as The Enchanter's Plant or Herb of the Cross, vervain was a favourite of the Druids, who used it in divination, and for the consecration and ritual cleansing of the body, spirit, and of sacred spaces.

It is best known as a protector. Roman soldiers carried it with them into battle as a good luck charm, and homes were also sprinkled with an infusion of vervain to keep out evil. This is its use in sin eating practice too: as a guard against negative thoughts and actions by bringing peace to the mind and spirit and protection for the soul.

A simple vervain tea can be made from 1-3 teaspoons of the herb left to steep for fifteen minutes. For a tea that will reduce anxiety and cure insomnia and fitful sleep, three teaspoons are blended with two of chamomile, and one of mint. Hot water and honey is added and the tea is drunk before bedtime.

Hyssop: The final sinner's herb is actually a blend which creates, according to Adam, "not an entirely pleasant taste – though more so than some others. But its job is not to be pleasant. It is to restore balance to the soul by opening the patient to Grace".

It can used as a restorative if you have had a bad day or been exposed to unwholesome energies and feel 'unclean' or stressed as a consequence.

The formula is made by adding together one teaspoon of hyssop, ½ teaspoon of coriander, ¼ teaspoon of dried rose petals, and a pinch (1/8 of a teaspoon or less) of rue. It is important to leave out the rue if you are pregnant , however, because it has a physical effect on the reproductive system.

Add the herbs to a pint of water with three dashes of cider vinegar and bring it gently to the boil, then leave it to simmer for ten minutes. Strain and decant the liquid and add a table-spoon or two of honey. Drink it while warm.

The key ingredient in this brew is hyssop, which is known as 'the Holy Herb' because of its ability to bring healing in whatever form is required. It is an aid to greater alertness, but also relaxing and good for treating nervous exhaustion. Coriander has similar properties for the relief of anxiety and insomnia.

EXPLORATIONS: THE PLANTS OF GOD
She took them to a place which is still called the Physician's Dingle (*Pant y Meddygon*), where she showed them the virtues of the plants and herbs which grew there, and taught them the art of healing.

W Jenkyn Thomas, *The Lady of the Lake*, from *The Welsh Fairy Book*

POWER PLACES IN NATURE
As the quotation above from the story of *The Physicians of Myddfai* suggests, there are power places in nature where we can tune in to the spirit of plants and trees and learn the secrets of the Otherworld. These may be dingles (wooded dells or hollows in the landscape), forests, or mountains and hillsides. Most shamans have one or more of these they can retire to in secret, to rest, recuperate, and take power, and which act as a sanctuary for the transmission of healing wisdom from the soul of nature to theirs.

The way to find these places is to dream them with intent: to ask the spirits to show them to you, in other words, through your dreams, journeys, or through 'happy accidents', such as when you open a book and see a photograph of somewhere that lifts your heart. Once you know these places in this way through the calling of spirit, then visit them, in ordinary reality if you can, but, if not, then in your journeys.

Many Irish healers undertake *turas* or pilgrimage once a year to their special places of power, to simply sit and dream, taking sustenance from the Earth. They may stay for a day or a week or a month, with no agenda but to share the company of a spirit greater than their own and to receive whatever gifts of healing and wisdom are given.

Some conduct ceremonies, but many do not; they simply relax, open, and accept whatever spirit is gracious enough to provide.

It is a good and beneficial practice to 'sit out' like this, as this practice may also be known. And, of course, take a gift with you for the place which is your ally.

THE SHAMANIC DIET

If there is a particular plant or plants that you would like to know better, and which you sense contain healing for you, one way to develop your connection with it is to *diet* it.

The process begins by spending time with the plant. Sit with it, look at its shape and colours, touch its leaves, inhale its scent, taste it. Explore, play, and have fun. Then, with its permission, gather some of the plant, dry it, and store it ready for your diet.

There a number of ways to diet any plant, but the easiest is to make an infusion in water or a tincture by macerating the herb in alcohol (vodka is best for this as it has little by way of flavourings and colour) and leaving the bottle in a cool dark place for a few weeks, giving it a shake every day.

The advantage of tinctures is that they last for many months so the plant is always available.

Last thing at night and first thing each morning before breakfast, drink a cup of the tea, or three teaspoons of the tincture, and, after a week or so you may start to find your life taking on the qualities of the plant as your spirits mingle and blend. You may also find the plant spirit appearing in your dreams, and that these become deeper and more meaningful.

When you feel that a connection has been made between you in this way, begin a practice of journeying to its spirit two or three times a week, so it can reveal more of itself to you and offer you guidance on healing or lifestyle.

Most shamanic diets are followed for three months or so, dieting one plant at a time and keeping the rest of your food intake quite bland and alcohol-free, apart from the tincture itself. A daily practice of stillness and meditation is also good as it opens up the mind and heart so you can hear the whispers of spirit.

After three months you may wish to diet a different plant, in which case you should cease your practice with the first, although you will wish to reconnect with it periodically (as you will with all your plant allies) after your dieting ends.

In this way, you continue to learn from it.

MAKING FLOWER ESSENCES

Flower essences are another way of dieting plants, by preparing their blossoms as an infusion in water which is energised by the sun for solar herbs, or moon for lunar herbs, then diluted and preserved in brandy.

Anything from one to six flower heads are normally collected from the plant to create each essence, but connect with, or journey to the spirit of the plant you have chosen so you are guided on how many flowers you need for any essence you have in mind.

Once you have collected the flower heads, place them in a bowl with two pints or so of pure water.

Put this in your garden beneath the light of the moon or sun while you make your prayers and requests to nature for the healing properties of the flowers to be released into the water. Take the bowl back inside after this and let the water stand for three hours.

Add brandy, in a ratio of about 50:50 alcohol to essence, and decant the mixture into clean glass bottles. Fit the lids and label them with the name of the flower and the date.

These can now be taken back to the garden if you wish (or to your power place in nature) for a final infusion of sun or moonlight and prayer.

These are your 'mother tinctures', from which you can produce your essences by decanting them into smaller glass bottles or vials.

CHAPTER 3

SIN EATING AND HEALING
WITH NATURE

I have learned
To look on nature, not as in the hour
Of thoughtless youth; but hearing oftentimes
The still, sad music of humanity
William Wordsworth, *'Tintern Abbey'*

To understand the place of plant healing within the sin eating tradition, an appreciation of two concepts is necessary: the nature of illness and its cure, and the importance of the elements and their place in the body. We look at the first of these concepts here, and the second in the chapter that follows.

'SIN' AND THE SHAMANIC UNDERSTANDING OF ILLNESS

The meaning of sin, in the way it was used in the Welsh tradition, is closer to its medieval than its modern Christian usage. *Sin* may be an old English translation of the Aramaic word, *khata*, which was used in archery and meant 'to miss the mark': the centre of the target. When that happened, the scorekeeper would yell out the word "sin!" – not as an accusation or term of reproach, but as feedback to the archer so he could adjust his aim.

Sinister is a word from around the same period which was used in Heraldry, and refers to the side of a shield on the wearer's left, the side which covers the heart.

Putting these two associations together, we might say that when we sin, we miss our targets. We usually go 'left of the mark' because we naturally tend to follow 'the path of the heart', which is on the left of our bodies.

The symbolism of this for soul work and healing is twofold: firstly, that no one is born evil; we all act from love and follow the same heart path. But unless we practice so that our aims are true, our love can sometimes be misguided. Practicing our love is exactly what the Welsh Saint David advised when he preached that we should "do the little things" and perform small acts of loving kindness every day.

Secondly, sin is a feeling in our souls which tells us that something is wrong; that we have not given of our best; that we are out of resonance with love.

It is, in other words, energy within the body that provides us with feedback similar to that of the scorekeeper in archery and allows us to adjust our behaviour so we get closer to the mark.

Shamans the world over perceive illness or 'dis-ease' in a similar way: as a sign of disequilibrium or disturbance in our inner state. From their perspective, imbalances usually result from two specific causes:

- **Spirit intrusions:** where forces external to us find their way into our energy system, often through our assimilation of them from the people around us. These result in some form of discomfort which heralds the soul's understanding that it is being drawn away from love.

   Someone in an abusive relationship, for example, may feel that the other person has so much power and control over them that their souls have been swallowed and filled with the needs of others to the detriment of their own.

   In the Welsh tradition, this intrusive energy is the 'sin'.

- **Soul loss:** where traumatic events, such as abuse, like that above, result in the loss of some of our life force so we no longer feel joy or a healthy desire for engagement with the world. At the root of this feeling is the knowledge in our souls that love is not being served.

Both of these forces tend to act together, and can lead to spiritual imbalances and physical illness, so that someone with an 'intrusive spirit' inside them (or, that is, an energy which is not naturally their own but an imposition from others) can find that part of their soul becomes eroded and is lost.

They might then become ill because their heart is simply not in living. Their illness is another message from their souls that something needs to be corrected for their spiritual and physical health. If they do not make this correction, problems will arise as increasingly obvious messages that something is not as it should be.

If they make the necessary changes, however, their souls can begin to recover and return to normal. Adam called this process atonement: *At-One-Ment*; the soul coming back into balance.

The role of the shaman or sin eater is to aid the patient's return to this state and to good health, not by dealing with the *symptoms* of disease, but by addressing the *cause*, removing the energies which are making the patient ill, and restoring his vital spirit.

To illustrate this process, let's take the example of a middle-aged man with hypertension who goes to a healer for help. This is a real case study, incidentally, based on a shamanic consultation with an actual client.

Hypertension, commonly called 'high blood pressure', is a serious medical condition where blood pressure is chronically elevated to a systolic level of 140mnHg or greater, and a diastolic level of 90mmHg or greater. In many cases (known as 'essential' or 'primary' hypertension), doctors can find no medical reason or organic cause for the patient's condition. Nevertheless, it can still lead to strokes and heart attacks, and even moderate elevations in blood pressure can mean a shortened life expectancy. At severely high levels, where blood pressure is 50% or more above average, the patient can expect to live no more than a few years if they are not treated.

An orthodox doctor would be inclined to immediately treat the symptoms, possibly using the anti-coagulant drug warfarin to thin the blood and reduce the pressure on the heart. The use of drugs like these is not without its own problems and side-effects, however (warfarin, for example, is also used as a rat poison). But, more fundamentally, the doctor's approach is not geared towards rectifying the cause of the problem (and, in fact, the cause is considered relatively unimportant); it is to clear up the visible symptoms by suppressing them with drugs, a process which also makes the patient dependent on the drug and the doctor.

Shamanically speaking, this is a perverse state of affairs, and not without irony, since all diseases of unknown physical origin are, by definition, matters of the soul which arise due to a lack of power within the sufferer. Instead of helping the patient regain his power, however, the first requirement of drug therapy is that he gives away more of it by relying for his healing on the doctor and the pharmaceuticals he must take.

(Incidentally, numerous studies have now shown that simple garlic can lower blood pressure by <10mmHg, as a natural alternative to drug therapy. This may be enough to bring the patient back to full health in cases of mild hypertension. But this again is treating the symptom, not the cause. [25])

Studies in America show that, for economic and social reasons, physicians interrupt their patients within 10 seconds of meeting them, in order to gather data or prescribe pharmaceutical treatments, so it is unlikely that the cause of an illness will ever be known in the scramble to 'fix it' by getting rid of (or masking) the problem. Hence, the reliance of the medical profession on drugs, which may sometimes be excellent symptom-suppressors, but do little to effect a cure because they have no role to play in removing the cause of the illness.

Shamanic consultations are different. Firstly, the healer might spend an hour or more listening to his patient before any intervention takes place at all. This approach is rooted in the tradition of confession, where the patient is allowed to speak freely and unburdon himself so that the fears, anxieties, and energies he is holding on to can start to be released and, through this, the healing of the soul can begin.

'Confession' is a universal approach among shamans, which really amounts, in many cases, to simple respect and empathy for the patient, instead of maintaining a distance between them.

In the Celtic traditions, the shaman becomes, not a remote clinical expert, but the *anam cara*: the 'soul friend' who will listen with sympathy and without judgement, no matter what the patient needs to say. In the Andes, the same approach is known as *placitas*, defined by one healer as a "heart-to-heart, soul-to-soul" consultation. [26] It makes perfect sense, since the patient who is suffering knows his illness better than the healer who is not.

While an *anam cara* consultation takes place, the shaman will not just be listening, but calling on his guiding spirits to be present in the room as well, so he can take advice from experts more knowledgeable than himself. He will also be quietly scanning the patient's energy so he can see with greater clarity the imbalances present and how they might be healed. In this, he will be guided by his intuition in a way that medical doctors, with their dependence on scientific procedure, professional distance, and data, cannot, and, indeed, are not allowed to do. Only when the shaman has truly understood the nature and spiritual cause of the problem, will he begin his treatment.

So let us return to our example again, of the man who arrives with high blood pressure.

As a result of the *anam cara* consultation or confessional, the healer now knows that his patient lives alone and hasn't really taken care of himself for some years. He sees little point in doing so, since there is "only him" and "no-one to share things with", so why bother cooking for himself, eating healthily, or taking time out to watch the sunset, walk on the beach, or relax in nature? His emphasis on 'not taking *care*' of himself is significant, both in the words he uses and the symbols and moods they evoke.

Things weren't always this way, he continues. A few years ago he was "full of life" and felt loved and loving, but since his wife died and his children have grown up and gone their ways, he feels alone.

All the time he has been speaking, the patient has not once mentioned the physical symptoms of his illness, but only how he feels.

This is his soul's recognition that, at the root of his problem is a lack of love, of people to care for and be cared for by.

All the warfarin in the world will not cure a broken heart. It is *love* which is fundamental to our survival and quality of life. Indeed, government medical advisors in the UK now say they can accurately predict a shorter life expectancy for anyone who answers no to the questions, *"Does anyone love you?"* or *"Do you feel loved?"*

In the case of this patient, it is not insignificant that his illness (hypertension) is a disease which affects the heart.

In response to the lack of love in his life, the patient tends to throw himself into his work, and, in his time of aloneness, smokes and drinks too much, and eats foods of convenience, which are comforting but stodgy and processed, with no life force of their own and few health-giving properties.

As a defence against loneliness and pain (because love goes away), he has also become withdrawn from others and nervous about trusting them, which adds to his isolation.

PLANTS THAT HEAL THE HEART

From this background, and on the basis of the shamanic plant medicine principle that 'like will cure like' (ie. a plant with the same qualities or spirit as the sufferer will be able to understand and heal his problems), two herbs that immediately suggest themselves to the shaman are poison-nut and lovage. [27]

Poison-nut comes from a tree that was brought to Europe from south-east Asia in the 15th century. Two hundred years later, it was discovered by physicians to have a stimulating effect on the nervous system, and to help with emotional problems.

In 1805, it was proved by the pioneering homeopath Samuel Hahnemann as a treatment for these and more spiritual ailments to do with love, and is now widely used as a homeopathic remedy in the form of *Nux vomica*.

Nux vomica is suitable for workaholic, perfectionist, personalities who thrive on challenges and drive themselves to excess. The typical patient who will benefit from it is sensitive, 'nervy', wounded by criticism (but very self-critical), and, because of this, sometimes irritable and stressed. He is absorbed more by the mind than the emotions, which he may find threatening, and tends to lead a solitary, anxious, life, putting distance between himself and others.

While he can be attentive, committed, and deeply loving of others, he is often very unloving towards himself. He may also find it difficult to express his feelings openly, and often does not like to be touched. His relationships tend not to last very long because of this and because of his dependence on his inner life.

To compensate for the emptiness he feels, the 'Nux personality' often overloads his body with experience, and may have a high sex drive, consume too much rich food, coffee, or alcohol, or abuse drugs. The effect of this can be to create tension, depression, and sleeplessness, which exacerbate his problems.

Lovage is another herb that suggests itself in this treatment, because its spiritual intention is to do with love and especially, with the ability to love oneself.

Although science maintains that 'loving qualities' are nothing to do with this plant, and that its name, which suggests this connection, is simply a misunderstanding, lovage has been used successfully by herbalists for 600 years to heal problems of the emotions arising from lack of love, and is also the basis for aphrodisiacs and love potions which bring the attentions and affection of others.

In medieval texts it is referred to in the old French as *luvesche*, as love-parsley, and as love-ache. Culpeper called it a "herb of the Sun" because of its warming and tonic qualities, which also aid the circulation.

These plants may certainly help, therefore, with this patient's immediate situation, and bring more love and vital energy back into his life.

Arriving at this stage might mark the end of a consultation with a typical herbalist, but the plant shaman will wish to explore further, and establish the origin or spiritual cause of the problem. For the sin eater, remember, everyone is born perfect and in a natural state of connection to the love which pervades all things and the flow of spirit that arises from it.

If we have become blocked and unable to feel and express this love – if we are 'sinners' and 'miss the mark' – it is due to external forces or patterns we have learned from others which have caused a corruption of our souls. These forces are spirit intrusions.

Influences like these arise from the behaviour of people towards us when they have also become disconnected from nature and out of balance with the natural world. They then express their longing for connection in a neediness that can manifest as anger, jealousy, or control; all of which are forms of misguided love.

If we are young, unformed, or vulnerable, the patterns these people and their intrusive energies set up in us through their behaviour towards us can become a force so intense that it comes to guide our actions and thoughts, as if we have lost our sense of self and will.

The Irish poet, Yeats suggests something similar when he writes that:

The borders of our minds are ever shifting
And many minds can flow into one another...
And create or reveal a single mind, a single energy. [28]

To understand the nature of this intrusive energy, to establish where it has come from and who has sent it – and then to know how to remove it – the shaman must establish a connection with his healing spirits and the soul of his patient. This, again, means opening to nature.

In the Scottish Highlands, one way of doing so was through a divinatory technique called *frith*, which is usually performed by the seer or *fritheir* at sunrise on Monday morning, following a period of fasting and prayer.

He must be barefoot and bare-headed and walk three times around his hearth fire, then go to his front door and, with eyes closed, stand on the threshold. He then opens his eyes and notes what he sees. He circles the house and repeats the exercise twice more, until he has a sense of the mood of things.

Some signs or omens are held to be good luck or *rathadach* and some bad luck or *rosadach*. Lucky omens may include seeing a man looking towards him or an animal standing up. Bad omens include a woman walking away, a pig with its back to him, or a crow flying towards him.

From these pieces of information, the *fritheir* is able to use his poetic imagination to develop a story in his mind which contains all three omens and, in some way (not necessarily literally), explains the circumstances of his patient's life.

Others may conduct divinations with runes, with ogham sticks, or with leaves which are thrown onto a table so their patterns can be read. A leaf which lands in the centre of the table and which represents the patient may be surrounded by others, for example, as if he is trapped or forced against his will. If another leaf has fallen onto the central leaf it might suggest undue influence or an element of control from someone in his life.

The 12th century writer, Gerald of Wales, wrote of diviners called *Awenyddion* ('Awen-inspired Ones') who entered trance by sitting and quietly tuning into or meditating on the gateway to the Otherworld and who then, eyes closed, would deliver their prophecies and diagnoses in verse.

The *Awenyddion* were practicing a form of the shamanic trance or journey we have looked at in earlier chapters, and this is the most direct and obvious method that a healer might use to connect with his patient and the intrusive energy within him: by closing his eyes, calling to spirit, and journeying into his soul.

Doing so in the case of the patient in our example revealed images or spirit information – later confirmed as true – of a childhood spent in isolation as the only son of elderly parents who had made a pre-retirement move to a secluded house in the country, taking him with them, but leaving him alone for most of the time. His spirit had been patterned to live a solitary life and, having little opportunity to interact with others, he had become wary of outsiders and unpractised in relationship skills.

His parents were also set in their ways and fastidious and

picky. They demanded the best from him but were critical of his successes as well as his failures, and praise was fleeting and rare. He learned as a consequence to be driven, to always be set on new goals and achievements, not living in the present, and critical of himself.

A child's soul is malleable, and these pressures around the boy moulded his spirit, giving him little choice but to become the man he had.

Sometimes in Celtic myth, invasive energy, stemming from family dramas, secrets, and shames, is referred to as *geis* or *dihanedd*. It is a form of curse, challenge, or purgatory that the hero of the tale is drawn into against his will or without his permission.

Such was the case of the warrior Lleu, one of the central figures in the *Mabinogi*.

Lleu was placed under a *geis* or *dihanedd* by his mother, Ariahrhod, from the moment of his birth, as a form of revenge against her brother, Gwydion, for the incest and rape he had committed against her which led to Lleu's birth. Like many actions taken in anger and bitterness, Ariahrhod's curse was misguided since it had little effect on Gwydion, but drew the innocent child into a parental drama which was not of his making. The curse was that he might never have a name or a wife, that he would be a bastard and loveless forever.

Despite the odds, Lleu managed to overcome his curse and, according to *The Battle of the Trees*, was able to lead a good and "kindly" life, as a strong and respected warrior:

Mynavc boedyl Minawc ap lleu...
Bu gwrd y bwrd yg kateu

Kindly was the life of Mynawg ap Lleu...
Mighty was his thrust in battles

Effectively, however, Lleu's whole life was spent as a pawn in his mother's battle of power and spite, and in fighting for his own identity and freedom.

Dramas like these are probably repeated to some extent in everyone's life, though rarely, we must hope, as hurtfully as Ariahrhod's curse against Lleu. The curses our parents may reap on us instead are their words, actions, and beliefs which form an insidious energy that comes, in some way, to infect us and drive our lives, leading us into unconscious behaviour which is harmful to us in some way.

Martin, a student of mine, suggests how geis – in the real world rather than myth – might have a subtle but present impact on anyone, when he talks about a client who came to him for hypnotherapy because of anxiety problems she was having.

> Joanne had a frantic air about her, always doing something and unable to relax. We tried a few sessions aimed at relaxation but made little progress until I asked her under trance: "Why can't you stop *doing* and just *be* instead?"
>
> She looked puzzled for a moment and then said: "Because dad says I'll never amount to anything without hard work".
>
> You could see the penny drop. Dad hadn't ever said she must work hard 24/7 (and probably hadn't meant that either) but her subconscious had taken his phrase literally. That was her *geis* and by realising this she had taken the first step in breaking it.

REMOVING THE SIN

To remove intrusions like these and bring a patient back to health, the shaman will first try to negotiate with the intrusive spirits to leave. As Adam once pointed out, spirit intrusions are not evil, per se, but often innocent themselves and unaware that they are harming anyone; they are simply trying to live. They have their own identity, presence, and existence, and to remove them by force would be like God removing us from the face of the Earth on a whim or with selfish intent. This, too, would be a sin.

If, however, the spirit will not leave, then the healer must remember that his first duty is to his patient, and remove the intrusion anyway. This is called spirit extraction and can be performed by stinging the patient with nettles, paying attention to "the corners and angles" of the body – the backs of the knees, elbows, back of the neck and belly – where intrusions tend to congeal. The nettle stings draw the intrusions out, where they can be safely washed away.

A more straightforward method is to simply grab the intrusive energy with the hands and cast it away. Alexander Carmichael describes this process in the *Carmina Gadelica*. In one charm, tellingly called *Exorcism of the Eye*, which is to remove the powers of 'the evil eye' (ie. energy sent by another with the intent to harm), the shaman first states his purpose, gathers power for himself, and warns the intrusion of his plans so its spirit can leave peacefully if it wishes:

I will trample upon the eye
As tramples the duck upon the lake
As tramples the swan upon the water
As tramples the horse upon the plain.

If this does not work, to gather further power and inform the intrusion that battle is about to commence, the healer continues:

Power of wind I have over it
Power of wrath I have over it
Power of fire I have over it
Power of thunder I have over it...
Power of the heavens
And of the worlds I have over it.

This is a list of natural forms such as fire and thunder (others mentioned in the whole incantation are moon, sun, stars, and storms), which are the shaman's allies and from where he draws his power. Following this, he pulls the intrusion from his patient's body and gives it back to nature, hoping that it may find a home there, and knowing that it is, at least, gone from his patient and broken into a thousand pieces so that it cannot easily reform and seek him out again:

> A portion of it upon the grey stones
> A portion of it upon the steep hills
> A portion of it upon the fast falls
> A portion of it upon the fair meads
> A portion of it upon the great salt sea...

Once again, these are all aspects of nature, which the shaman knows to be the greatest healer of all and the transformer of all energies.

In a variant of this charm, called *Spell for Evil Eye*, the shaman has a more forceful intent: to scatter the negative energy and return it to its sender. After his opening warning that "I will subdue the eye, I will suppress the eye, I will banish the eye", he grabs it and casts it away in pieces, but this time sending it to:

> Who so made to thee the eye
> May it lie upon himself
> May it lie upon his house
> May it lie upon his flocks
> May it lie upon his substance
> May it lie upon his fatness
> May it lie upon his means
> May it lie upon his children
> May it lie upon his wife
> May it lie upon his descendants.

With the energy gone, the shaman now turns his attention to power retrieval – the return of life force and good energies to the patient's soul.

This may be done, as part of the shaman's journey, by connecting with a natural force, such as a tree, a plant, or a mountain which wishes to help the patient by offering a part of its transformative spirit to him. The shaman collects this good energy and blows it into the patient's heart, returning it in the form of blessings which he might say out loud or direct silently to his patient's spirit:

Thou art the pure love of the clouds
Thou art the pure love of the skies
Thou art the pure love of the stars
Thou art the pure love of the moon
Thou art the pure love of the sun
Thou art the pure love of the heavens...
Thou art whiter than the swan on miry lake
Thou art whiter than the white gull of the current
Thou art whiter than the snow of the high mountains
Thou art whiter than the love of the angels of heaven...
Thou art the gracious red rowan
That subdues the ire and anger of all men.

Another form of retrieval is mentioned in the *Carmina Gadelica* for soul loss.

It is called, significantly, a charm for *Displacement of the Heart* following "fright" – a sort of emotional trauma which can lead to soul loss.

The shaman goes (in reality or in his journeys) to "a stream under a bridge over which the living and the dead pass" (ie. symbolically, a threshold place between worlds, where his patient's soul-energy is trapped).

There, he takes water from the stream in a wooden *cuach* (cup), along with three stones from the stream; one shaped like the head, one like the heart, and one the shape of the body. These are placed in the cuach with the water to carry them home, where they are heated on the fire until they are red hot.

They are then placed, one at a time, into the water, and the shaman observes which of them gives off most steam as it cools. If it is the heart stone it confirms that it is, indeed, the patient's heart that is affected (ie. that there is a lack of love in his life or that his heart is broken or blocked). This stone is then placed on his heart, the head-stone above his head, and the body-stone beneath his feet as the shaman prays over him and offers blessings. The spirit of the heart-stone which holds the patient's soul is thus empowered to enter his patient's heart and bring him love, strength, resilience, and protection against further wounding.

At the end of a healing like this, which has involved rational, as well as spiritual, consultation, confession, the removal of negative energies, and the calling back of the soul, the patient has been empowered, knows the cause of his illness, and has been given the energies he needs to overcome it. He also has the herbs (poison-nut and lovage in the example quoted) to help his physical symptoms. More importantly, perhaps, he has been heard, honoured, blessed, and given suggestions for what he might do to ensure his well-being by seeking opportunities for love and to embrace what is meaningful. love. Not time spent away from the spirit on a never-ending quest to achieve, but a fuller engagement with life.

Healing methods like these were practiced in all the Celtic nations. In Ireland, they can be seen in the approach of two legendary healers: Biddy Early and the "faery doctor", Bridget Ruane.

THE PLANTS OF THE FEY

According to Lady Gregory in *Visions and Beliefs in the West of Ireland* [29]:

> In talking to the people I often heard the name of Biddy Early, and I began to gather many stories of her, some calling her a healer and some a witch. Some said she had died a long time ago, and some that she was still living. I was sure after a while that she was dead, but was told that her house was still standing, on the other side of Slieve Echtge, between Feakle and Tulla...
>
> It was a wild road, and the pony had to splash his way through two unbridged rivers, swollen with the summer rains. The red mud of the road, the purple heather and foxglove, the brown bogs were a contrast to the grey rocks and walls of Burren and Aidline, and there were many low hills, brown

when near, misty blue in the distance; then the Golden Mountain, Slieve nan-Or, 'where the last great battle will be fought before the end of the world'...

When I got back at night fall to the lodge in the woods I found many of the neighbours gathered there, wanting to hear news of 'the Tulla Woman' and to know for certain if she was dead.

I think as time goes on her fame will grow and some of the myths that always hang in the air will gather round her, for I think the first thing I was told of her was, 'There used surely to be enchanters in the old time, magicians and freemasons. Old Biddy Early's power came from the same thing'.

Biddy Early was born Bridget Ellen Connors near Kilanena, in 1798, but lived in Feakle, County Clare, at the time of her death in 1873. She was the daughter of John Thomas Connors and Ellen Early; and married four times in her life, but always kept her mother's maiden name, because her gifts, she said, were inherited through the female line. Her parents died when she was sixteen, whereupon she travelled Ireland, until she met and married her first husband, Pat Mally, when she was in her early twenties and he in middle-age.

Pat died in 1840 and she married again and moved to a cottage on Dromore Hill, overlooking a lake which became known as Biddy Early's Lake. By then she was called 'Biddy the Healer', 'The Wise Woman', or, simply, 'The Witch'.

She used scrying to diagnose her patients' illnesses by gazing into the Otherworld through the reflective surface of a blue bottle which showed her visions of their pasts and future. This magic bottle was given to her by her son, she said, who won it playing hurley for a team of strangers who vanished into the air as soon as the match was over.

A hero of the people, Biddy was opposed by the clergy, who tried to warn off anyone who visited her for healing. When that didn't work, in 1865 she was charged, in Ennis, with witchcraft, but the case was dismissed because her patients who were called to testify against her refused to do so.

In her healings, she said she was guided by the *sidhe* (pronounched *'shee'*) – the People of the Mounds, or The Lordly Ones; spirit allies and healers descended from the Tuatha de Dannan, who she saw and spoke to in an unknown language, and by the visions they revealed in her bottle. She died with this bottle beside her and, to ensure that it did not fall into the wrong hands, it was subsequently thrown into Kilbarron Lake, along with the secrets it contained.

There is a saying in Irish", writes Lady Gregory, that it is simple folk who are the true healers: *'An old woman without learning, it is she will be doing charms.'"*

Such was the case with Bridget Ruane, another of the faery doctors of Ireland.

I can't do all cures, though there are a great many I can do," Ruane told Lady Gregory. "I cured Pat Carty when the doctor couldn't do it, and a woman in Gort that was paralysed, and her two sons that were stretched. For I can bring back the dead with the same herbs our Lord was brought back with – the *slanlus* and the *garblus*...

It was my brother got the knowledge of cures from a book that was thrown down before him on the road... Maybe it was God gave it to him, and maybe it was *the other people*... He taught me a good deal out of it. So I know all herbs, and I do a good many cures, and I have brought a great many children home, home to the world – and never lost one, or one of the women that bore them. I was never *away* myself [ie. taken to the land of the fey], but I am a cousin of Saggarton [another Irish healer and seer], and his uncle was away for twenty-one years."

During his time away, Saggarton learned many lessons from the land of the fey and developed a deeply spiritual nature and an understanding of the souls of men and of the dead. According to Lady Gregory,

The soul,' he says, 'was the breath of God, breathed into Adam, and it is the possession of God ever since. And I could never have believed there was so much power in the shadow [or dark side] of a soul, till I saw *them* [the lost souls of the dead] one night...

They tempt us sometimes in dreams – may God forgive me for saying He would allow power to any to tempt to evil. And they would destroy the world but for the hope they have of being saved. Every Monday morning they think the Day of Judgment may be coming, and that they will see heaven*. Half the world is with them. And when you see a blast of wind, and it comes sudden and carries the dust with it, you should say, 'God bless them', and throw something after them...

There never was a funeral *they* were not at, walking after the other people. And you can see them if you know the way – that is, to take a green rush and to twist it into a ring, and to look through it. But if you do, you'll never have sight in the eye again.

"I asked her [Ruane] to teach me some of her fragments of Druids' wisdom, the healing power of herbs," writes Lady Gregory, "So she came another day, and brought some herbs, and sorted them out on a table..."

These are some of the herbs and their uses that she learned:

- *Ddwareen* (knapweed) and *fearaban* (water buttercup): To strengthen and heal the bones, when boiled with sugar as a tea.
- *Corn-corn* (tansy) and *dub-cosac* (lichen): Both good for the heart when boiled and drunk; the latter also for a "sore [and broken] heart".
- *Atair-talam* (chamomile): "The father of all herbs". For peace. When it is cut and pulled up, you must always use "a

---

* This reflects the belief, among some healers, that the faery are the souls of sinners whose deeds on Earth were not bad enough for hell but not good enough for heaven. They are therefore caught between worlds until they repay their debts or the Day of Judgement arrives when all sins will be forgiven.

black-handled knife".

- *Camal-buide* (loosestrife): To keep "all bad things" away.
- *Bainne-bo-bliatain* (wood anemone): For headache, the leaves are placed on the head as a cure.
- *Lus-mor* (mullein): The only herb which is "good to bring back children that are *away*" [ie. taken by the faery]. "There's [also] something in green flax I know, for my mother often told me about one night she was spinning flax, before she was married and she was up late, and a man of the faeries came in. She had no right to be sitting up so late, they don't like that. And he told her to go to bed, for he wanted to kill her, [but] he couldn't touch her while she was handling the flax."
- *Slanlus* (plantain) and *garblus* (dandelion): Heal-alls, which "would cure the wide world". "Sunday evening is the best time to get them" although, in general, "Monday is a good day for pulling herbs, or Tuesday, not Sunday. A Sunday cure is no cure". "Seven Hail Mary's I say when I'm gathering them, and I pray to our Lord and to St Joseph and St Colman. And there may be *some* [faery or spirits] watching me, but they never meddled with me at all." One reason for this close observation by 'the other folk' is that dandelion is also "the herb for things that have to do with the faeries... when you'd drink it for anything of that sort, if it doesn't cure you, it will kill you then and there".

The greatest healing power of all, however, and the greatest protection against soul loss and spirit intrusion, was to maintain a healthy connection to nature, which is "the direct expression of the divine imagination", in the words of the Irish poet, John O'Donahue in his *Anam Cara: A Book of Celtic Wisdom*. [30]

One enjoyable, and health-giving way of doing so is simply to take a forest walk once in a while. That may be enough. Doing so, we fill our lungs with fresh, clean air – the gift of the trees – get exercise, and gain a sense of peace and union with nature. Through this we may also come to realise our place in the scheme of the universe and many of our trivial but stressful human concerns begin to disperse like morning mist, giving us back the seeds of our power. If you wish to combine it with a healing ritual, one method is to find a tree that calls to you, then sit down with your back to it and speak to it of your problems and sorrows. If you listen carefully, the spirit of the tree – the great transformer and gateway to nature – will provide the advice you need, while taking away your pains and giving you a new sense of power and purpose.

EXPLORATIONS: SIN EATING AND HEALING WITH NATURE

We place nine pure, choice gifts in your clear beloved face:
The gift of form; the gift of voice; the gift of fortune
The gift of goodness; the gift of eminence; the gift of charity
The gift of integrity; the gift of true nobility; the gift of apt
speech.
Traditional Irish blessing

ASKING FOR BLESSINGS

One of the most beautiful – and, often, most subtle and powerful – forms of healing for yourself or for others is a heartfelt blessing infused with the spirit of love.

Blessings feature often in rituals for health and well-being practiced by the shamans of the Scottish, Irish, and Welsh traditions.

Some can be short, to the point, and even blunt, like this one from Scotland: *'Lang may your lum reek'* – or 'Long may your chimney smoke', meaning, in essence, 'Long life and health'.

And this, even blunter, blessing for protection from Ireland:

May those who love us, love us
And those who don't love us, may God turn their hearts
And if He doesn't turn their hearts, may He turn their ankles
So we will know them by their limping.

While poetic inspiration is important to the pleasure we receive from hearing blessings like these it is not necessary, what *is* important is a connection to spirit so these gifts of Grace may be requested and given.

Walk out into nature on a pretty day, lie down by a stream, or in a sunny meadow, or woodland, and rest. Close your eyes and make an intention to meet with the spirits of that place, the faery, or "the direct expression of the divine imagination", in

O'Donahue's words – which is nature itself – to ask for a blessing which will help you to resolve some of the current issues you are facing, or ensure your greater success and highest good in your projects and undertakings. Let yourself dream your rewards and accept what is given. Write down the words that come to you so you have them as a blessing for your soul's journey.

A SPIRIT-GIVEN ALLY

The Scottish healer who collected stones for the heart, mind, and body, was given these three gifts by nature. The way to receive nature's blessings like this is to make a prayer to the spirits and then take a slow, relaxed, walk, keeping your mind and eyes open for objects and signs, so you are led to the places and things which can help you.

A prayer is a strong intention that things will be as you wish; in fact, that they already *are* as you wish, and you have just to notice it.

This expression of your intention opens your eyes to what is already yours and leads you to the gifts of nature that can help you with your healing.

Make your prayers and gather two or three of these gifts that cross your path – whether stones or feathers or flowers; or whatever calls you and wishes to be yours – and take them with you as you go.

Later, you can journey to their spirits to understand the healing they will bring you, and to learn how better to honour yourself and them.

CHAPTER 4

THE IMPORTANCE OF THE ELEMENTS

I praise my Father, my God, my strength
Who infused in my head both soul and reason
Who, to keep guard over me, did bestow my seven senses, from
fire and earth, water and air:
The mist and flowers, the wind and trees, and much skilful
wisdom has my father bestowed on me.
Taliesin, *Song of the Macrocosm*

To the Celts, the elements of Air, Water, Fire, and Earth are sacred
allies, as this oath, sworn by Conchobar, King of Ulster, suggests:

The sky is above us and the earth below and the sea all about
us. Unless the firmament with its showers of stars falls down
upon the earth, or the earth bursts asunder in an earthquake, or
the blue-bordered furrowy sea flows over the hair of the earth,
I shall bring back every cow to her byre and yard and every
woman to her home and dwelling, after victory in the battle.[31]

In Conchobar's words, all of the elements are represented: Air (the
sky), Earth, Water – "the blue-bordered furrowy sea" – and Fire –
the firmament "with its showers of stars". There is no deeper vow
or witnesses more sacred and important.

The elements were held in such high esteem because, in combination, they make up everything that is. Just as trees and plants are
their expressions – the breeze that scatters their seeds (Air), the
Water (rain) and Fire (sun) that feeds them, and the Earth which
holds them – so are we, and so is everything.

Taliesin writes that his senses were formed from "the elements
and sub-elements" and in the quotation which opens this chapter
he names them: Fire, Earth, Water, and Air. There is also a fifth

element: Spirit, which is a quality and a place within and outside of us, far away and near at hand. In Celtic literature it is sometimes described as a mist, a place beneath the waves, within the sidhe mounds of the earth, or on the islands of the Western Sea.

This spirit is the Otherworld-within-us, variously called *Tír na mBeo* (The Land of the Living) *Tír na nÓg* (The Land of Youth) and *Mag Mell* (The Delightful Plain) – a country where there is no sickness, aging, or death, and happiness lasts forever.

In the Irish *Immrama* – tales of great voyages – the hero sometimes finds this land by sailing a crystal ship to the Blessed Isles of the West, or sets out on a quest, during which a strange mist descends on him. After adventures which change him forever, he returns victorious to his home, believing that a short time has passed, only to find that a hundred years have gone by.

As metaphors, these tales tell us that when we are connected to Spirit we enter a timeless place of health, vitality, and happiness. To reach it, the four elements within us must be in balance so we can draw from the "strength", "skilful wisdom", and "soul" that Taliesin describes as the gifts of God.

The sin eater, Adam taught that in a healthy human body, all the elements should be present, balanced and flowing freely throughout our systems, with each one correctly aligned and in its rightful place of origin in the body. These places are:

- **The head:** Air originates in the head and circulates from the throat to just above the crown.
- **The heart:** Water originates in the heart and circulates from the throat to just above the solar plexus.
- **The solar plexus:** Fire originates in the solar plexus and stomach.
- **The legs:** Earth originates in the legs and circulates from the hips to just below the feet.

Each of these elements represents a different quality within us, which is animating and energising, allowing us to live a happy and healthy life which is filled with Spirit.

Air

Air (*aer*) is the element of thought, intuition, inspiration, the intellect, the dreaming self, and the unconscious. It is the medium through which we hear the whispers of Spirit and gain instruction and knowledge. Everything great in the world arose from this element, since nothing which is made can be designed or built without first having an idea, a vision, or a dream of it. Once this inspiration is given, the powers of the conscious and skilful mind – the use of reason, intellect, and expression – carry it into being.

The Celts were headhunters who revered the severed head as a source of spiritual power and the seat of the inspired soul. Paul Jacobsthal of Christ Church, Oxford, writes in his book *Early Celtic Art*: "Amongst the Celts the human head was venerated above all else, since the head was to the Celt the soul, centre of the emotions as well as of life itself, a symbol of divinity and of the powers of the other-world."

The severed head is referred to in many Celtic myths, such as that of *Sir Gawain and the Green Knight*, where the Green Knight picks up his own head to keep its essence safe after Gawain has cut it off, and in the legend of the hero Bran the Blessed, whose head continued to speak and provide counsel from the spirit world for seven years after it was removed. Bran's head is now buried, in the Tower of London, where it protects the British Isles from invasions.

A person with good Air energy will have access to these mythic realms, to their unconscious and the cauldron of inspiration it represents. They will be able to find novel ideas, solutions, and the creativity to dream the world that they want for themselves, as well as the ability to 'see it through' by focussing and holding a vision for their futures. The brow represents this capacity for focus and is the point of vision in the body, where the dreaming self meets the rational mind and we can see our futures ahead of us.

A person low on the Air element may be directionless and unable to visualise a future. He may seem confused, unclear and unable to find his truth, or conversely he may be too dependent on the rational aspects of the mind, out of touch with Spirit, so locked into the habits of intellectual thought that he is too anxious to achieve much at all.

Water

Water (*uisce*), at the place of the heart, is the element of love and the emotions. In a well-balanced energy system, and in a person who has had good life experiences and relationships, it is a place of brightness, represented in Irish myth by the magical Sword of Nuada, which knows justice and truth. Nuada means 'mist' or 'cloud', and symbolises the qualities of Water in their rightful place in the body.

Truth and justice are also represented in the story of Cormac, who was given the gift of a silver branch from a sacred apple tree by a mysterious grey-haired warrior who vanished as soon as it was given. When Cormac shook the branch, a mist enveloped him and he was lulled to sleep by the music of leaves.

He awoke in the Land of Promise, where only truth is known. At its centre stood a fountain surrounded by nine hazel trees which dropped their seeds into the water. He was taken to this fountain by faery maidens, who bathed him in the waters and gave him a magical gift: a cup of truth, which would shatter if three lies were spoken in its presence, so that Cormac would know falsehood from honesty. He returned with this gift and became a great leader of men.

Sacred waters, to the Celts, are usually associated with goddesses, many of them healers and wisdom-keepers, who know the truth of the universe: that all is love. In Ireland, Holy Wells are dedicated to Brigit, and rivers are deified by goddesses, such as the Boyne, named after Boann, the mother of Brigit.

A person low on the element of Water can be recognised by their lack of the qualities of healing and wisdom that these deities represent, and they may also be struggling with issues of truth and justice in their lives.

Since Water characterises the emotions and opens a person to love, those who lack it may appear distant, indifferent, or unfeeling. Inside, however, they are highly emotional and they may carry the wounds of love at a deep soul level. There may be much grief and sadness within them, but they might not even be aware of it since their feelings are deep-water mysteries, unfathomable and remote. Their sadness still affects them, though, and may leak out in displays of grief or anger (often a mask for sorrow), for which there may seem no apparent cause.

Fire
Fire (*teine*) is found in the solar area and is the element of power and passion. In a well-functioning energy body, if the head (Air) is the place of our dreaming, where new ideas and visions are formed, and the heart (Water) is the place where these ideas are filtered through the truth that we know and the love that we feel, the solar plexus is the place from where we take action in the world to make our dreams a reality.

Oíche Shamhna (or Samhain, on October 31) is one of the principal festivals in the Celtic year and the time when the harvest was gathered in and cattle would be slaughtered to provide the tribes with winter food.

Bonfires were central to these festivities and the bones of slaughtered cattle would be used to feed the flames. From this 'bone fire' each family would light its hearth fire, bonding the tribe together. Often bonfires would be lit alongside each other and the people, and their cattle, would walk between the flames to purify themselves.

Thus, Celtic Fire represents purpose, intention, passion, new beginnings, and the celebration of life. As part of the healthy human spirit, it symbolises lust, enthusiasm, courage, virility and power.

A person with low Fire energy has little enthusiasm for himself, for others, or for life. It is as if they have given up, because there is little pleasure to be gained from doing anything. Those lacking Fire may feel as if their will is gone, and they may also carry guilt, shame, or feel themselves inferior to and put upon by others.

Earth

Earth (*an domhan*) is the energy that runs from the hips to the base of the feet, and represents all that is secure and dependable. It is our stability, our under-standing, and our ability to walk out into the world with the dignity and confidence to put our plans into action.

In Irish tradition, the element of Earth is symbolised by *Lia Fail*, the Stone of Destiny. Standing on the Hill of Tara in County Meath, it was given to the people by the Tuatha De Danann so that the true King would be recognised by its cries of joy. It served as the coronation stone for all the High Kings who, by their rule, brought good fortune and stability to the land.

A person low on the Earth element most likely feels unstable in some way: confused, lost, insecure, alone, or ungrounded; unbalanced, and unable to move forward with his life. He may feel 'stuck' as if in mud.

Because of their impact on a patient, healers need to know when these elements are low within a person and how to restore them by using the appropriate herbs to empower them and get them flowing correctly again. There is a *materia medica* of these plants at the end of this chapter.

More commonly, these elements are not at such a low ebb that they are lost completely, but they become misplaced, so that Air now takes the place of Fire, or Fire takes the place of Water, and so on.

These misplacings create unhealthy effects on the mental, emotional, spiritual, and physical selves. Too much "fire in the head", for example, may lead to compulsive thinking, anger or frustration, and disconnection from love and spirit. Within the physical body, it may give rise to excess heat, which can lead to skin complaints, migraines, heart problems, or strokes.

The chart below gives an idea of the problems that may come from misplaced energies.

Element	Normal place in the body	Normal function	Ruled instead by	Effect on the patient
Air	Head	Dreams, visions, and ideas	Water	Emotions rule the head. New ideas are frightening and thoughts of the future bring panic. Thinking becomes 'clouded' or too fluid, resulting in problems of faith, belief, and spiritual connection; (possibly) leading to madness.
			Fire	Thoughts and ideas become obsessive, compulsive, irrational, or driven. Thinking becomes overly-analytical, critical, judgemental, or angry.
			Earth	The person feels burdened or weighed down by confusions, lost, insecure, ungrounded, or keeps returning to the same thoughts over and over again, as if stuck in a cycle. This may also suggest an inability to forgive or to allow themselves to be forgiven.
Water	Heart	Love and connection	Air	Emotions are suppressed and thinking takes the place of feeling, leading eventually to expressions of grief.
			Fire	Anger and 'letting off steam' may be common when Fire and Water mix, resulting in and arising from unresolved issues or stress. Too much heat can lead to the heart 'burning out' as a result of its greater effort to feel, leading to cardiovascular problems.

			Earth	Earth in the place of Water produces 'muddy' feelings, confused emotions, and indecision. The weight of Earth on the heart may also bring problems as the heart has to work that much harder.
Fire	Solar Plexus	Passion, will, commitment	Earth	The weight of Earth on the lungs may produce feelings of claustrophobia, panic, or breathing problems.
			Air	Fire is inflamed by Air, adding to the intensity of unpleasant thoughts, such as jealousy and dissatisfaction with life.
			Water	Repressed emotional pain and rage may arise, masked by sorrow.
Earth	Hips, legs, and feet	Stability, balance, the ability to move forward	Air	Difficulty in finding focus, ideas too rooted in the physical world, leading to a lack of imagination and ineffective solutions.
			Water	Emotions are deeply repressed, creating feelings of 'being a victim' or attracting the energies which *make* one a victim and lead to constant 'bad luck'.
			Fire	Can feel like the ground beneath one's feet is being burned away or that the body is on fire, physically or symbolically. Fire in Earth is the elemental condition in many zealots and martyrs.

The discovery of the four elements and their effects on our energy is credited to Empedocles, a 5th century BCE Greek *Iatromantis* (seer and shaman) and *magos* (priest-magician), who was esteemed as a philosopher, prophet, and healer. His *Tetrasomia*, also known as the *Doctrine of the Four Elements*, provides a framework for understanding the elements, although Empedocles, as a "root cutter" or plant shaman, actually called them 'roots' (*rhizai*) rather than elements.

According to Empedocles these roots are spiritual essences which manifest in the body and respond to the natural energy of the universe, which is a delicate balance of love (*philotês*) and strife (*neikos*). When the elements become imbalanced or mis-placed, therefore, it is because we are out-of-flow with love and have opened ourselves to pain.

In sin eating philosophy, this inability to flow with the love of the universe arises from 'Origin-al Sin'. Simply, we have forgotten our origins in God and become lost in a world of forms and illusions.

Healing comes from restoring balance and the memory of our divinity.

THE HEALING INTERVENTION

A typical healing within the Celtic tradition might be performed, first by *gazing* the patient, allowing the eyes to go out of focus as you stare into the patient's energy field and 'tune in' to their spirit, to establish where the elements are in their body. This will often produce symbolic images in the mind of the healer, who may see a pool of dark Water in the patient's stomach, for example, where Fire should be present instead. Or the healer may see a heart which is inflamed and full of Fire, where Water energy should be. The healer can then use his hands to push these energies back to their rightful positions.

This seems to have been the approach of the renowned Irish healer, Valentine Greatrakes. Greatrakes was born in Waterford on February 14, 1628, and went on to become a lieutenant in Cromwell's army, and, later, Clerk of the Peace for County Cork. In this role, in 1661, he was involved in the trial of Florence Newton for witchcraft and felt no aversion to the use of torture as a 'witch test' to prove her guilt.

Two years later, however, at the age of 34, Greatrakes had a change of heart and became inclined towards 'witchcraft' himself, following what he later called "an impulse or strange persuasion... which did very frequently suggest to me that there was bestowed on me a gift of curing." [32]

His first patient was a young boy suffering from scrofula, a form of tuberculosis affecting the lymph nodes. Greatrakes wrote that: "I laid my hands on the place affected, and prayed to God for Jesus' sake to heal him and within a month ... he was perfectly healed." His fame as a healer spread quickly and he was inundated with people visiting him for healing. His method was to stroke his patients with his hands, moving their energies to their appropriate alignment and rebalancing the elements in their bodies. As a result of this, he became known in Ireland as The Stroker. He continued as a healer until his death in 1682.

Although their approach was the same, other Celtic healers used slightly different methods. Adam, the sin eater I learned from, used a bundle of leaves to brush his patients, tracing a route from the head to the feet on either side of the body to remove negative energies, and then paying more attention to the elemental areas, brushing them with the leaves, as if 'painting' them back into shape.

As a final blessing for his patients, and to anchor their energies where they belonged, he would rest his hands on their crown and pray for them:

Peace of the singing summer breeze be upon you
Power of the dreaming hills
Wisdom of the hawk and the endurance of mountains
Grace of the protective wings and whispered breath of angels.

Finally, patients would be given a herbal drink to take home and use each day, to keep their energies in place until they were fully integrated back into their body and the tonic was finished. Some of the elemental herbs used in mixtures like these can be found in the next section.

Healing takes place when the world of Spirit (the shaman's allies and plant helpers) meets the world of the physical (the shaman himself and his knowledge of the patient and his needs). Spirit and healer must work in partnership, since the spirits are not of this world and cannot heal effectively without a physical agent for their cures.

The shaman, meanwhile, cannot heal without the assistance of spirit and inspiration.

The attitude of the spirits and the shaman are both important. There must be openness, love, and a desire to help in their intentions towards the patient or else the magic cannot work.

As the stories of Brigit and the first coming of the plants, and *The Physicians of Myddfai* illustrate, love and compassion are the greatest healers of all.

There is another Welsh tale, in some ways reminiscent of Jack Fox and the Leprechaun, which shows that while personal gain may be a legitimate and understandable reason for our contact with spirit (it is, after all, a fundamental reason for seeking healing in the first place), it should never be the primary motivation for those who work with spirit.

There was a Welshman who came to London to sell his herd of cattle. With the few coins from the sale in his pocket – and carrying a staff of hazel in his hand - he was looking at the sights of the city, when he noticed a man watching him with a curious look in his eye. The two got to talking.

"Where are you from?" asked the Welshman.

"I come from my own country," said the stranger. "And where did you cut that stick?"

"Does it matter?" asked the Welshman with amusement.

"Indeed it does," the stranger replied, "for there is a great treasure buried at that spot and, if you take me there, I will show you magic that will cure all ills and make you a man of wealth."

The Welshman realised that only a sorcerer could make a promise like that, and grew afraid because he knew that sorcerers gain their power from the Devil. But the stranger was persuasive and the lure of money was great, and so presently they set off together.

They journeyed to *Craig y Dinas*, the Rock of the Fortress, in Wales and when the Welshman pointed to the place of the hazel, they began to dig.

Before long, they came upon a large, flat stone, and lifting it, they found steps leading downwards, and a narrow passage with a door at their end.

"How much do you want things for yourself?" the stranger whispered.

"Enough," replied the Welshman.

And so they went together into the cave beyond the door. A great army slept there; thousands of soldiers, side by side, as far as they could see; each clad in armour, and carrying a shield and shining sword. In the middle of them was a round table at which their leaders slept, and, at the head of it, a King's throne.

"Arthur's warriors, with Arthur at their head, and Excalibur in his hand," said the stranger in a hushed voice. "They have slept here for a thousand years, waiting for the time when the ailments of Wales would again demand their attentions."

The stranger and the Welshman rushed towards the heaps of gold that lay next to the table; the wealth of Arthur which would fund his next campaign.

Filling their arms with as much as they could carry, they turned to leave. But the stranger was clumsy in his greed and spilled coins on the floor. At the sound of it, the warriors leapt to their feet and the voice of Arthur rang out: "Who has woken us? Has the day come?"

"No!" cried the stranger. "It has not. Sleep on!"

Arthur was standing now and saw the two who had woken him. "It is only two gold-seekers who want power for themselves," he said. And, with a wave of his hand, he dismissed the thieves from his sight.

The Welshman awoke to find himself once more in London, the few coins from the sale of his cattle jangling in his pockets and his heart filled with regret at what he had tried to do.

Many times he tried to make his way back and ask the forgiveness of Arthur, but though he searched the whole of Wales, he could never find the cave again. He remained poor and humble, a farmer for the rest of his days.

EXPLORATIONS: THE IMPORTANCE OF THE ELEMENTS

She found me roots of relish sweet
And honey wild, and manna dew
And sure in language strange she said
I love thee true.
John Keats, *La Belle Dame Sans Merci*

Healing begins with diagnosis, with understanding from our patients and spirit allies what has gone wrong and why. We can then work with the appropriate plants to help those who come for healing. Two diagnostic methods are confession and gazing.

THE TREE OF ANAM CARA

One ritual of confession makes the tree an *anam cara*: a soul friend you can tell your cares and concerns to and unburden yourself of the energies which are holding you back from life.

Find a place in nature and a tree you feel drawn to, making sure that you are alone for this. Take with you four bowls, some water, and a lighter or matches.

Place one of the bowls in each of the four directions around the base of the tree. Leave one empty (so that it is filled, in effect, with Air), fill one with soil (Earth), one with Water, and in the last put a little kindling and a few dry twigs so you can make Fire.

Now sit quietly and meditate for a while on what it is you wish to say.

When you are ready, speak it out, with the tree as your witness. Feel, as you do so, that a weight is being lifted from you and that negative associations and energies are leaving your body to be absorbed and transformed by the tree.

When you have said enough, walk the tree in a clockwise direction (the direction of increase and power), pausing at each of the bowls in turn for a moment of reflection about all that is good in your life and where your positive energies will take you.

Say out loud: "I am blessed by Fire" (strength, passion, and courage). And as you stand before the bowl, take a little of its heat by stroking your hands through the flames and resting them over your solar plexus.

Then move on: "I am blessed by Water" (good and positive emotions). Sprinkle water from the bowl on your heart.

Again, move on: "I am blessed by Earth" (grounded and secure). Brush a little of the soil down your legs, from the hips to the base of the feet.

Finally, come to the last bowl and say: "I am blessed by Air" (clear thought and vision). Dip your hands into the bowl, as if you were gathering substance and rub it over your brow and crown.

When this is done, walk away without looking back and begin your new life with an intention for positive change.

The next day you can return to collect the bowls.

If you are a healer, this is a beautiful ritual to share with your patients who are looking for a fresh start and a better outlook on life, by walking with them to a tree they are called to, and explaining the practice to them.

Give them a little time alone with the tree to make their confession and then, if they want you to, join them as they walk the circle of the elements so you are a witness for their commitment to change.

One of my students undertook three confessions for herself and expressed her experience like this. It shows, I think, the potential and healing that is possible, and the way that the process deepens every time.

As I worked through each confession, I discovered that it slightly changed.

I had originally started out with pain, anger, frustration and hurt before slowly turning to love, surrender and forgiveness. I found my initial words to be clumsy but as I worked with each confession, energies and words flowed more freely and I felt more in control and in focus, as if I was gently releasing the anger which was allowing me to tap into the other emotions which lay hidden under the veil of red hot energy, i.e: the hurt and misunderstood child. Tears flowed freely throughout the entire session helping release all the pent up energies which have been held for so long. I also felt that the people I was focusing on and relating to could hear me. I had a very clear image of them/their soul listening and releasing.

During the confession, I realised that although I had apologised a long time ago for the delivery of some untimely words, I had not actually released that person because I was still carrying the guilt.

When owning my guilt during this exercise and then working through the self-loathing and denser energies, I felt the cord tug and then gently release and knew that this person would also experience a lightness, even though they may not understand what it was.

During this entire exercise, I saw colour and vibration as well as the individual faces concerned. I felt a great sense of release and relief and I feel a lot lighter within myself and my energy-field. What a great tool!

GAZING THE ELEMENTS

Gazing is the practice which allows us to see the configuration of energies and elements within a patient's body.

Begin by slowing down to the pace of nature – watch the wind in the trees on a quiet day: *that* is the pace of nature. Breathe deeply with slow and regular breaths, and allow your eyelids to slightly close and your eyes to go out of focus, as if you were drowsy and ready to sleep.

As you gaze in this relaxed way at a person before you, take your attention first to a point about two inches above their heads and you will become aware, in the peripheral vision at the bottom of your line of sight, of a hazy outline to their body, which you can trace all around them, from head to toe.

Now scan across their body, up and down, in the same way, remembering the places in the energy system where the elements should normally be found: Air at the head, Water at the chest, Fire in the belly, Earth in the legs.

As you gaze at each of these points, thoughts, suggestions, or images will pop into your mind. If these are not appropriate to the element in the area of the body you are gazing (for example, if there is Fire in the head when it should be Air), the person you are with requires healing to realign the elements of their body.

A MATERIA MEDICA OF ELEMENTAL HERBS

These plants regulate and balance the elements of the body. To know them better and experience their effects for yourself, choose one or two and diet them for a time, noting how you feel. Your diet should also include a period of journeying to the spirit of the plant, so you form a bond between you and add to your understanding.

Air Plants

Air plants work on the mind and draw energy back to the head so that it can circulate effectively and does not stagnate, giving rise to thought-related problems. They include:

Pansy: Shakespeare's Ophelia says of this plant that it is "for thoughts". Its name comes from the French, *pensée*, which also means 'thought'. It was so named because, following *The Doctrine of Signatures*, its flowers resemble a human face, which, in August, bend forward as if deep in reflection on matters of importance.

Pansy will help clear the mind and relieve sorrows and bad memories, hence its other name, *heartsease*. For these reasons, it has been traditionally prescribed in medicines and spells to help with ending the removal of negative energies from the mind, and for protection, purification, and vision.

In the 'language of the flowers', popular in the 1800s, the three colours of pansy, purple, white and yellow, represented memories, loving thoughts, and 'keepsakes'. The latter might be regarded, positively, as joyful memories which need to be brought back to the surface, or, negatively, as repressed memories which may have to do with guilt or forgiveness. The patient's confession will help you to clarify which is more likely, but pansy can be used to bring healing to both, resulting in peace of mind.

Primrose: Charles Darwin described how the shape and arrangement of primrose flowers served an evolutionary function by ensuring that only a determined and long-tongued insect could reach the honey at their base, and by probing for the nectar, pollen is collected along the way and transferred to other flowers when the insect moves on.

Symbolically, primrose is an aid to healing the deeper problems of the mind, such as grief or betrayal. Through primrose's healing, we can also find our sweetness and honey, and move on to more fertile ground.

Primrose has sedative and relaxing qualities, and has been used successfully by herbalists to help patients with insomnia, nervous or hysterical disorders. Gerard recommended it for depression and wrote that "Primrose Tea, drunk in the month of May, is famous for curing the phrensie" (melancholy, fear, sorrow, or 'distraction'). In modern herbalism, a tablespoonful of root infusion may also be prescribed for these conditions, as well as for nervous headaches.

Vervain: The Enchanter's Plant, Holy Herb, or Herb of Grace, vervain is one of the sacred plants of the Druids, who used it, according to Gerard, for "witchcraft and sorceries". The Romans called it *hiera botane*, or 'sacred plant'.

It has sedative and relaxant qualities, and is good as a nerve tonic to heal melancholia and depression by strengthening the nervous system and calming the mind, while soothing away tensions and stress.

The Welsh Physicians of Myddfai prescribed vervain to prevent bad dreams, by hanging it around the neck or drinking its juice before sleep. In the modern day it is still used in Bach flower remedies to relieve mental stress, aid sleep, and help an uptight patient to relax.

Vervain is best avoided in pregnancy, however, as it is a uterine stimulant, although it can be taken during labour to help contractions.

Water Plants

These work chiefly on the emotions and tend to be 'watery' or moist themselves, apart from the first, club moss, which is very dry and is used to soak up excess water and 'dry out' the emotions.

Club moss: *Lycopodium* (its botanical name) means 'wolf's claw', and was given to it because of its claw-like stems. In shamanic animal symbolism, the wolf is the hunter, using its heightened senses and advanced skills of tracking to find its prey. It is also the healer; its sharp claws and teeth having the ability to tear away illness.

This is also the function of club moss on the emotional level: to track down the causes of negative emotions and remove them from the body, so they no longer block the flow of Water energy.

The College of Physicians, in 1721, recommended club moss mixed with black pepper as a cure for hydrophobia: *fear of water*. As a metaphor for illness, 'hydrophobia' represents the fear of facing our sadness, the Water in our bodies. The effect of club moss is to make grief manageable and reduce its impact on the body.

Nowadays, the main part of the plant used in treatments is its spores. A diluted powder of these will help reduce the swelling of blood vessels in the heart, and on a symbolic level, therefore, will help the emotions to flow without obstruction.

Club moss is also used to heal heartburn, on a physical or a symbolic and emotional level, and will soothe the pain of inner sorrow.

Other functions of club moss also tend to be 'watery'. The Druids called it 'Cloth of Gold' and used it as a diuretic.

Irregular menstruation, oedema, and dysentery are other Water complaints it has helped. It is not to be used while pregnant, however, or over long periods of time.

Water lily: This herb takes its botanical name *Nymphaea* from Nymphe, the goddess of springs, and even today, it grows where nymphs are said to play. Some believe that water lilies *are* nymphs, in fact, disguised as flowers to escape the amorous attentions of humans. For this reason, in medieval Germany, lilies were regarded as symbols of purity, and have been used by herbalists for their *anti*-aphrodisiac qualities. Culpeper says of them that they "stop lust".

One of their uses for the emotional centre is to bring a sense of calm perspective on things, especially for patients who demonstrate an over-reliance on short-term thrills, excitement, sexual conquests and adventures, but who are looking for enduring love, and so have become 'their own worst enemies'.

Water lilies are also good for people who attract relationship dramas and those who act out their emotions to gain control over others (and who may therefore be disconnected from their true feelings, insecure, or lacking in love).

Willow: The willow tree is known as the tree of love and harmony. Commonly called 'the weeping willow', the bark of this tree contains salicin, the active ingredient of aspirin. These pain-killing properties work at a spiritual as well as a physical level.

It is one of the herbs best-loved by the moon and the fey, and was used by poets to contact the faery, who would whisper words of love and inspiration in their ears.

The Druids used it for enchantment, healing, and to bless friendships and bring love and peace. Its branches were hung up to protect against magic and negative energies sent by others, or bad feelings and painful memories in relation to love.

Willows are often planted around cemeteries and used to line graves because of the protection they offer the dead. Symbolically, they are good for emotional endings and to nurture and protect those who feel 'dead inside'.

Willows make excellent allies if a patient needs to 'get something off his chest' or to share a secret he finds it too painful or shameful to reveal. If he makes his confession to a willow (see the first exercise in this section), the energy will be released from his emotional system and given to the keeping of the tree so his secret is safe forever.

Fire Plants

These strengthen the will, passion, commitment, and the ability to enjoy life and feel fully a part of it, as well as regulating heat in the temperament which can give rise to destructive (and self-destructive) forces like anger. They include:

Garlic: There is an early Christian myth which says that garlic first grew in Lucifer's footprints as he left the Garden of Eden. In the sin eating tradition, Lucifer is the light-bringer, and the serpent of Eden was the deliverer of wisdom who led human beings to the Tree of Knowledge and to consciousness of their divinity. If this Christian myth is true, it therefore makes garlic a blessed plant indeed, and it has long been regarded this way in Europe, where it is often used as the first protection against evil and a potent ally in the practice of magic.

It has both a cooling and a heating effect on the Fire in the body. It cools things down when the passions are too inflamed and agitated, or when a stubbornness of will has taken over from common sense and consideration for oneself and others. Conversely, if Fire is missing from the body, garlic will stoke the flames and get it flowing again. It can also heat the body in a way which, like the practice of 'fighting fire with fire' to put out forest blazes by deliberately setting the undergrowth aflame, can release rage in a dramatic and explosive outburst. Once this willful anger is gone, the sorrow hiding beneath it can be expressed, bringing the system back into balance.

Hibiscus: Widely respected for its ability to renew vitality and vigour, hibiscus also tempers the will so that it does not lead to control issues or the need to get one's own way, which can mean conflict with others. Its effect is to encourage feelings of intimacy, responsiveness, and friendship, by warming the heart.

It is regarded as bringing "dignity" to the emotions and a respectful and appreciative approach to relationships. It has a gentle, nurturing, warmth that counteracts the excesses of Fire which stem from insecurity and can lead to the need to constantly prove oneself, or to the smouldering acidity of regrets and recriminations.

When the will has been damaged and a patient has 'closed down' through the impact of emotional wounding, exploitation, or abuse, hibiscus will gently support them and aid their return to power and the ability to give and receive affection.

Its physical effects include the ability to relieve fever, aches, and pains, and, in tests, it has been shown to lower blood pressure and cholesterol levels, while its antibacterial properties can help to combat cystitis.

Cinnamon: One of the first spices, its fragrance was highly valued and it was often burned during spiritual rites and funerals.

Its principle quality is to aid circulation, physically, and of the Fire element around the body and energy system, so that genuine power, warmth, and zest for life is restored. It is especially beneficial in moving 'stuck' Fire energy and for people who need to rekindle vigour and passion.

A traditional 'medicine' recipe using cinnamon is hot spiced cider:

¼ cup of brown sugar
1/8th teaspoon of allspice
½ cinnamon stick
1/8th teaspoon salt
1 pinch of nutmeg
1 large orange, quartered with peel
1 large apple, quartered with peel, and
1 pint of apple cider

Warm the ingredients in a saucepan over a medium heat for five minutes, then allow the mixture to cool and remove the fruit and spices, unless you are drinking it immediately as a winter punch. It can be cooled, bottled, and, stored in a fridge for a day or two, to be reheated when desired or drunk cold.

Earth Plants

These are grounding, supportive, and help us move forward with purpose. They include:

Oats: On the Isle of Man, on February 1, (Brigit's Feast Day – *Laa'l Breeshey*,) before people retire to sleep, there is an old custom of Making Brigit's Bed. A sheaf of oats is dressed in the clothing of a woman and a bed is prepared for it beside the hearth, with ashes from the fire sprinkled round it. The woman of the house cries out three times, "Brigit come; Brigit is welcome". In the morning, if

Brigit's footprints are present in the ash, it is an omen for a good and prosperous year, with healthy and fertile crops. [33]

Oats are 'of the Earth' and represent stability, prosperity, fruitfulness, and rewards through the application of purpose to achieve our desires. They are especially helpful for patients who feel trapped in the past, locked into unfulfilling cycles and habits, or who find it difficult to move on and achieve new growth in their lives.

For these reasons, oats have traditionally been used to treat depression, nervous exhaustion and debility, to give resilience and strength, and to fight anxiety and panic attacks. They bring a sense of calm to those who are over-active or so driven and confused that they start a million projects without completing any of them, and may feel that they have achieved very little and their lives lack meaning. Oats have a sedative effect on people like this and settle their energies down so they can focus on one thing at a time and see it through.

They have also been used as a natural aphrodisiac (hence, the expression 'to sow wild oats'). Studies confirm these benefits through their ability to raise testosterone levels and increase muscle excitability.

Used externally, by adding them to bath water, for example, oats can help with dry and inflamed skin conditions, acne and eczema, by lowering the Fire in the body (like throwing soil on a blaze to put it out), and then cleansing and rejuvenating the system.

Dieting oats is simple. Porridge can be made, for example, by boiling an ounce of oatmeal in three pints of water, adding honey or raisins for flavour.

An oat tincture can also be made by adding four ounces of ground oatmeal to a pint of alcohol, and leaving it for a day or two. About half the liquid is then decanted off, and the rest is evaporated down to leave half a fluid ounce. Both parts are then added together to produce an effective tonic for the nerves.

Ivy: Poet's crowns were made from ivy leaves, as was the wreath of Bacchus, the Greek god of wine, to whom the plant is dedicated; and it is said that binding the head with ivy will prevent intoxication and wild imaginings. It gifts are those of *focussed* inspiration (rather than drunken and confused ideas) and the ability to 'keep one's feet on the ground'.

Its yellow berries are used by some herbalists, following *The Doctrine of Signatures*, to treat patients with jaundice, the yellowing of the skin when too much bilirubin is present in the blood.

Shamanically speaking, this is of interest, since negative energies (or bad spirits) find their way into the blood and often make their presence known through blood disorders and by the appearance of the sufferer. A jaundiced expression makes a person *look* sick and is a signal that intrusive energies are present, or perhaps, that the patient is holding on to things from the past which are best let go. Ivy helps discharge these energies to the Earth, and this is reflected in one of its modern uses as a circulatory compound to assist the removal of waste products from the skin.

(Ivy is, of course, poisonous, so although it is not taken as a herbal remedy, it can be used homeopathically – the remedy is *Rhus tox* – rather than ingested as a herb.)

Oak: Oak is a symbol of strength, perseverance, and measured growth. They are slow-growing trees (often not exceeding 20 inches in diameter in 80 years), but immensely powerful and highly revered. Their botanical name, *Quercus robur*, reflects this and is derived from the Celtic words *quer* (fine) and *cuez* (tree).

In England, 'Gospel truths', oaths, and promises were made beneath their branches and expected to be kept.

The oak therefore signifies the powers of fortitude, endurance, and commitment to our journeys, which may be difficult, but, if we stay grounded and move forward at a measured pace, are sure to produce results.

As we make this journey, however, we must also watch our boundaries so we remain true to ourselves and are not manipulated by others, or too open to their influences and energies.

This 'boundary function' is another quality of oak. Historically, they provided resting places in the old ceremonies of 'beating the parish bounds', where, once a year, people would walk the boundaries of the parish and stop beneath oaks to read passages from the Gospels and ask for blessings.

By dieting oak, the boundaries of our spirits are similarly protected and the blessings of oak will strengthen us.

CHAPTER 5

WAYS OF WORKING WITH PLANTS

We bathe your palms
In showers of wine
In the crook of the kindling
In the sacred elements
In the sap of the tree
In the milk of honey
Traditional Irish blessing

When the warrior, Cormac, was taken to the Land of Promise, the first blessing he received from the fey was a bathing ritual which took place in the Fountain of Knowledge, whose waters were fed by the fruits of the hazel tree.

Rituals like these, in floral waters and plant-infused streams, are common in Celtic lore, just as they are in the shamanic traditions of many other cultures, as ways of working with plant spirits.

Because shamans work with the essence and energy of plants, their spirits and compassionate intentions, it is not necessary for a patient to ingest them as 'medicines'.

Their real healing comes from the changes they evoke in that patient as the spirit of a loving and intelligent consciousness enters his soul and begins to affect him from within. Being in contact with this spirit, or in its presence, is all that is required; it is not necessary to consume it.

For these reasons, shamans have evolved other ways of working with plants, which are unlikely to be encountered in any other healing discipline.

Among them, all of the elements are represented, so we find Water cures and blessings, Fire ceremonies and sweatlodges, Earth rituals, such as burials, and healings which employ the element of Air as a medium through which the plant spirits work their magic, such as the use of incense and perfumes as a form of benediction.

WATER CURES

In *Welsh Herbal Medicine,* David Hoffmann writes of Druidic healing practices:

> For internal and lingering complaints they mainly used the cold bath… with the administration of herbs. Great use was made of water from certain wells, due to their specific mineral and spiritual properties. [34]

Herbs and baths were used for a variety of purposes, including anointments, the prevention and cure of illnesses, and for the procurement of love, good luck, and friendship; in fact, according to Hoffman, herbal baths could be used "to obtain all that the heart desires".

The fact that water was important to the Celts is known from the number of votive offerings that have been recovered from wells and pools. At the shrine of the water goddess, Coventina, at Carrawburgh on Hadrian's Wall, for example, more than 13,000 coins, as well as pearls, carvings, and other items have been found, all of them left by people paying homage to, or requesting the blessings of, the goddess.

That they received these blessings is evidenced by the sheer number of offerings. One does not return to a 'doctor' if that doctor cannot heal.

Large quantities of metalwork have also been recovered from bogs, lakes, and rivers; including tankards, weapons, and cauldrons, which the author, Barry Cunliffe, writing in *Iron Age Communities in Britain,* notes is: "Impressive for the high quality of the material. One must suppose a surprisingly high percentage of society's wealth was dedicated to the gods in this manner." [35]

It is clear that the Celts took the power of water very seriously.

Cauldrons also hold water, of course, and to the Celts, they were symbols of regeneration from the Land Beneath the Waves, like the vessel of the Dagda, which satisfied all hunger and restored the dead to life. In this, they are symbolic of the womb, the protective matrix of life.

The world's most famous cauldron is probably the one found in a peat bog near Gundestrup in Demark in 1891. Dating from the 2nd or 1st century BCE, this silver vessel has a capacity of 28 gallons and is highly decorated with symbols and icons. One of its plates depicts Cernunnos, the horned Lord, who grips a serpent in his left hand and is surrounded by animals, including a stag with antlers similar to his own, dogs, cats, and a human figure riding a dolphin.

In another part of the cauldron, warriors pass in procession on either side of the Tree of Life, watched over by a dog (the herald of death) and a giant who immerses the men head-first into a Cauldron of Regeneration. Restored to life, they leave the scene on horseback led by a snake, echoing the words of the Gwynfydolion: "We are serpents", and the observation made by the mythologist, Joseph Campbell, that the snake, in all shamanic cultures, represents: "Immortal energy and consciousness ... constantly throwing off death and being born again."[36]

Another famous cauldron, the Welsh Cauldron of Annwn, may be the forerunner of the Grail in Arthurian legend; a vessel which, in the words of Caitlin Matthews, in her exploration of the *Mabinigion*, enables us to "draw knowledge" and which is kept boiling by "the breath of nine muses"[37]. This is the cauldron of inspiration and wisdom, of healing and benefaction, and which aligns itself to the element of Water through these virtues.

Not all of the offerings made to Holy wells and springs were from people seeking well-being and blessings, however. At the Roman spring in Bath, in addition to around 16,000 coins and *paterae* (libation pourers), 50 curses were also found, in the form of lead sheets which were rolled up and cast into the water with a message of ill-will and misfortune inscribed on them. St Elian's cursing well in Clwyd, Wales, had its share of visitors with a similar intent, but here the victims' initials were marked on stones and dropped into the water.

In Scotland, the waters of Holy wells were known to quieten storms at sea, to cure the lame, bring sight back to the blind, restore the barren, ensure a successful harvest, and grant fidelity and happiness to lovers. The wells on the isle of Iona rejuvenated the old and provided protection and favourable winds for sailors.

At St Mary's Well, near Culloden, sick visitors came to drink the waters and tie rags in nearby trees to signify their healing. In return for their blessings, on May Day, young women decorated wells like these with wild flowers, in a ceremony known as 'well-dressing', to ensure the power of the waters to heal for another year.

Outraged by this, the Scottish Presbytery, in 1656, condemned practices like these as "abominable and heathenish" and demanded that they end.

They made the same condemnations and demands a hundred years later when their original outrage did no good at all to prevent people seeking the healing of the waters. Such was the power of these wells, that right into the 19th century, pilgrims still made supplications and offerings there, an unbroken tradition that had continued for more than three hundred years.

Islands – mythical or actual – which are surrounded by water, also have a place in the Celtic heart. *Afallon,* (or Avalon, the Isle of Apples), the magical lands to the West of Ireland, and *Insula Sacra,* or Britain, the Sacred Isle, which the Roman writer Demetrius described as "full of awesome gloom" are all examples of enchanted lands. In these countries between the waves, life is always good, the spring eternal, the harvest abundant, and plants, trees, fruits, and flowers are always delicious and plentiful.

Water is a healer and a gateway to spirit in its own right, then, and it becomes even more efficacious when combined with the power of herbs. Flower and herb baths are therefore frequently used in shamanic healing as a means of washing away unhelpful spirits, removing blocked energy, and receiving blessings and restorative powers.

In a ritual use of herb baths, a tub may be filled with water from a Holy well, spring, or other power place, with an offering left to the waters in return. To this is added the plants that the patient most needs for his healing.

The word *votive*, as in a 'votive offering' left at Holy wells, comes from the Latin *vovere*: 'to vow', and means a prayer, dedication, wish, or longing. To receive the healing waters, the patient must approach them in a votive manner, with a yearning for his needs to be met, and in the certainty that they will.

The shaman then pours the water three times over his head, sometimes asking the patient to turn as he does so – first in a counter-clockwise direction so that negative energies are removed, then clockwise to draw in positivity. During the final pouring the patient stands still and breathes in the blessings of the flowers.

Sometimes this bath takes place on the banks of a river or stream, so the energy removed from the patient will find its way back to the sea. All energy is simply energy, after all, and neither good nor bad in itself. What does not serve this patient may therefore benefit others who are standing even now on the banks of some other stream in a far-off country of the world, seeking the blessings of Water too. The stream will take it to them.

Floral baths do not contain large numbers of plants. Specific herbs or flowers are chosen according to the patient's needs. In prescribing them, the shaman may consider whether the patient requires lunar or solar qualities (or perhaps both), and then through the patient's confessions, narrow these down to one or two which are particularly beneficial. He will observe ritual procedures on his walks to gather these herbs, and may also diet or fast as he prepares them.

At the root of most people's problems, no matter how they manifest as illness, is a lack of love. People who have love and who love life are generally more resilient to disease and will fight to stay alive and enjoy life to the full. Those who lack love may feel that they have little to live for and be more inclined to let the spirit of illness take them. Two flowers that are usually beneficial to include in any flower bath, then, are rose, for love, and marigolds, because they are "bright like the sun".

The patient, having received the waters, may pat himself dry with a towel, but if any petals remain on his skin, he should leave them there so that their gentle energy can continue to infuse and uplift him. Remaining quiet, contemplative, alone or among people who love him, is recommended for the rest of the day, and the patient should be gentle on himself, and watch his dreams closely that night. In the morning he may shower off any remaining herbs and petals.

I know that the spirits hear us when we bathe in their flower waters. At a plant spirit workshop I led in Galway in 2006, we prepared a floral bath on a fine sunny day, which we were to take outside by a small stream that snaked down from the hills, amongst heather, grass, and wild rocky outcrops. We retired to the house to make ourselves ready for this ritual adventure and, just before venturing out again into the sunlight and gentle breeze, we prayed together for the blessing of the elements.

No sooner had we done so than, from nowhere, the skies opened and the rain lashed down in buckets, while a fierce wind shook the trees. We stood gazing at the crazed heavens for some minutes, not all of us delighted that we would soon be stepping into it, dressed only in bathing wear. It was, however, a necessity, and we opened the door to go outside. As soon as we did so, the rain abruptly stopped and the wind vanished all away. The sun came out again, as bright as it had been before, and in the sky above us, there were not one, but two rainbows. The ritual went ahead and we bathed under rainbows that day, the Water having answered our prayers.

Flower baths may also be taken as part of your normal bathing routine if you would like to try this practice. Decide on the qualities you need most in your life right now, and which herbs and flowers reflect this. If you are feeling a little stressed, you might choose soothing chamomile and refreshing mint to calm your nerves and release your worries, as well as rose and marigold for brightness and love.

Dried herbs are fine, but better placed in a muslin bag which is hung beneath the hot tap as the bath fills, or dropped into the bath instead of sprinkling them on the surface of the water, as their consistency can make them gritty at first, although they soften as they hydrate. You can also simmer the herbs in a saucepan for 15 minutes, then pour the water into the bath tub through a strainer.

The nicest way to bathe, however, is to sprinkle fresh petals and leaves on the surface of your bath, so you relax in a garden of herbs.

Whichever of these approaches you choose, explain your cares and concerns to the plants and the water and ask for their blessings as you add them, then step into the bath and soak.

Capture the loose herbs before you empty the bath and, next day, take them to a stream and offer them to the waters as a gift to the spirits for their help.

FIRE CURES

Sweatlodges are dome-like, spaces made of cloth or stone, heated by fire, in which people gather to sweat and purify themselves. Their modern equivalents are saunas, steam rooms, and Turkish baths. They are traditional to many cultures, where they play an important role as cauldrons of transformation in the healing of the community. All of the elements are present in the ceremonies which take place there in the hot Air of the enclosed Earth, where Fire and Water create cleansing steam. Chief amongst these elements, though, is Fire.

Celtic sweatlodges today often follow Native American lines, as tarp-covered domes of willow, which provide a place for rituals and healing. The ceremonies which take place within them are led by a shaman, an *eolai* (spiritual guide) or *turasaiche* ('one who makes a pilgrimage to the spirits'), who guides the prayers of participants and opens the doorway to the Otherworld so those present can find their way to well-being through spirit intervention.

The first Celtic sweathouses, however, were smaller, stone-built, beehive-shaped structures. The ones that survive in Ireland, such as those at Cornamore in Leitrim, Ballydonegan in Derry, and Skellig Michael in County Kerry, are rarely more than a few metres in height or diameter, and could not have accommodated more than three or four people at once. They have even smaller entrances, so that those who took part in ceremonies had to bow to 'the place of the fire' on entering. The doorways were then sealed with blankets or blocks of turf.

Often, these Celtic sweathouses are tucked away in natural and magical places, near streams or copses, and built into hillsides or banks, so they resemble small caves. They are covered with sods of earth, so they become a thing of nature themselves, and are almost invisible in the landscape.

According to Anthony Weir, writing in *Archaeology Ireland*, the Reverend Robert Gage of Rathlin Island (between County Antrim and Scotland's Mull of Kintyre), described sweathouses as:

> Constructed with stones and turf, neatly put together; the roof being formed of the same material, with a small hole in the centre. There is also an aperture below, just large enough to admit one person, on hands and knees. When required for use, a large fire is lighted in the middle of the floor, and allowed to burn out, by which time the house has become thoroughly heated; the ashes are then swept away, and the patient goes in, having first taken off his clothes, with the exception of his undergarment, which he hands to a friend outside.
>
> The hole in the roof is then covered with a flat stone and the entrance is also closed up with sods, to prevent the admission of air. The patient remains within until he begins to perspire copiously, when (if young and strong) he plunges into the sea, but the aged or weak retire to bed for a few hours. [38]

According to Weir, two cartloads of peat were required to heat the room for a sweating cure. Not everyone had the right to cut peat and when it was cut, it was required for heating the home, so two cartloads was extravagant to the poor of Ireland. Its use in the sweathouses suggests therefore that these rituals of healing were taken seriously indeed, especially as most of those sweathouses that survive are in the areas worst-hit by poverty.

Sweating is, of course, important for regulating bodily temperature and for removing toxins from the system at a physical and spiritual level. In the warm, moist, darkness of the sweathouse, closeness to God and rememberance of the womb also provides comfort and gives pause within a sacred space for reconsideration of what is important in life, and for reconnection with our purpose.

It is perhaps also more significant than it seems that peat was used for the fire. Peat bogs have had important ritual significance from prehistoric times, and evidence from Bronze and Iron Age peoples shows that they were considered the home of nature spirits. Votive offerings and even the bodies of animals and people offered in sacrifice have been recovered from the bogs of England, Ireland, and Europe. To sit in darkness in the ceremony of the sweathouse, is therefore to be truly among the ancestors and the spirits of healing.

Peat itself also has healing properties. It contains humic acids which strengthen the metabolism and is a preservative when absorbed through the skin. Some peat bogs have preserved bodies for millennia, including the so-called Tollund Man, Haraldskær Woman, and Lindow Man, all of which are at least 2,000 years old, but look as if they died just a few years ago.

There is really only one way to experience the healing of a sweatlodge, and that is to participate in one. A compromise that may be a little more accessible to you, however, is a steam bath, similar to the ones that Amazonian shamans use as a form of healing sauna for their patients.

To take a steam bath, fill a saucepan half full with water and add sprigs, leaves, or flowers of the herbs you would like to work with – the aromatics, such as lavender, rosemary, or mint are good for this. Bring the water to the boil on an open fire or a stove, and simmer for ten minutes, adding more water if you need to. Place the pan on the ground in front of you and use a blanket or poncho to make a tent over you and the pan, then bend into the steam. Stay there for as long as you wish, inhaling the aroma and the spirit of the plants, then take a cold water shower to energise you and close the ceremony.

AIR CURES

Although I was raised near Wales, Ireland is probably my favourite place on Earth. There is a different quality to the air. It feels as if you can *breathe* there; as if there is more space between the atoms. It is liberating, intoxicating, and it makes you feel excited by life.

The Irish mystic, George Russell, felt it too. "The air we breathe is like wine poured for us by some heavenly cup bearer," he wrote, his beautiful words capturing the reverence for the winds that all Celts feel who know it as the breath of God.

Perfumed air is a special Celtic fascination. The Welsh knew fragrant plants, whose healing was carried on these winds. As long ago as 430 BCE, they protected plant healing with potions, salves, and scents as one of 'the three civil arts' of Wales under the laws of *Dynwal Moelmud* (the other civil arts were commerce and navigation).

One of the plant shaman's healing practices in Wales was to 'bury an illness' beneath an aromatic plant. The sin eater, Adam, would sometimes do this, burying a bone with the name of a patient scratched on it beneath flowers or fine-smelling herbs. Each day he would pray near the plant and, with its permission, crush a few of its leaves in his fingers. As their perfume "made its way to God's nostrils", more of the patient's illness would also be released, making its way back to God as well, until the patient was free of it.

Like the Welsh and Irish, the Gnostic Christians of 100-400 ACE, believed that fragrance was the soul of a plant and a gateway to the spirit of the world. In their ceremonies for the dead, corpses were washed in perfume so that the soul would mingle with these fragrances and be carried into heaven.

Early herbal manuscripts, such as the Saxon *Leech Book of Bald*, written in about 900 ACE, also demonstrate a great reverence and deep knowledge of the fragrances of the natural world. Herbs, flowers, and perfumes were important to everyday life, and were used as as the tools of magic and medicine. Herbs offered cures for all sorts of ailments, and the sick were often 'smoked' with fragrant woods and plants to purify them and take illness away. Scented garlands were also used, with the dual purpose of decorating homes and bodies, and bringing healing through their perfumes.

These scented healers were used throughout Europe. Hildegard of Bingen, the visionary Abbess, (1098-1179) was a herbalist with a deep awareness of the connection between fragrance and healing. She is credited with the invention of lavender water, which she saw as a blessing from God.

Nowadays, aromatic pants like these can simply be hung in the home or car, or carried as a 'bouquet garni' for blessings and protection. But one of the enduring ways of working with fragrant plants, especially in rituals of healing, is as incense.

You can make incense of your own by collecting the leaves, roots, barks, or berries you wish to use, drying them thoroughly, and grinding them to a fine power with a mortar and pestle. Let this mature for a few weeks so that the aromas blend into each other, and you can then sprinkle it over charcoal and bathe in its healing scent.

An alternative is to make incense pellets by combining your herbs with dried fruits, such as raisins or prunes (about ½ a cup of fruit for every cup of incense) and blending it thoroughly in a food processor. Add a teaspoon of honey for every ¾ cup of mixture and knead it together, making small cones or balls of it. Let it dry for three weeks, turning it on a daily basis; it will then be ready to use by dropping it onto lit charcoal. Some healers put the pellets in sealed jars and bury them in the Earth for a year, so they receive the blessings of nature.

Breathing in the fragrance of incense is another way of dieting the plant so its spirit enters yours and, in the words of Taliesin, "the ardent soul shall be voyaging through the clouds with the children of angels". [39]

EARTH CURES

Fogous are underground ceremonial structures found in many Celtic lands. The name derives from *fogo*, the Cornish word for cave, although they are not natural constructions, but man-made from corbelled stone, tapering at the top and capped by stone slabs. In other parts of the British Isles and in Brittany, they are known as *earth houses or souterrains*. They also acquire local names that suggest their power and purpose, such as the one at Constantine in Cornwall, which is known as Pixie's Hall.

One theory as to their origin is that they were built as chambers for the initiation of shamans. This being so, it is significant that this ritual takes place beneath the Earth, as if the shamans were seeds themselves growing from the soul and the richness of nature, especially given the close connection between initiation, healing, and plants in all shamanic cultures.

In the Peruvian Amazon, ayahuasca shamans, as their final test, drink a massive dose of the visionary plant brew in front of their peers, then conduct a healing ceremony.

In Mongolia, sacred intoxication is practiced, during which the shaman-to-be must climb a tree and demonstrate the arts of balance.

In Siberia, the shaman, in trance, climbs a birch tree and cuts notches in the topmost branch, symbolising his ability to enter the sky-world.

In Haiti, the *asson* rattle, which is the symbol of shamanic priesthood, is given in the dark woods at night by a spirit called Loko. The name is likely derived from the word iroko, a tree which originates in Africa, from where many Haitians were taken as slaves, and, in that culture, represents the World Tree. The initiation of the shaman is, therefore, a form of home-coming, mediated by the trees and plants themselves.

It would be strange, then, in the cave or fogou initiations of Celtic shamans, if plants did not play a part. But in these rituals it is the shaman himself, by entering the womb of the Earth, who *becomes* the plant. He is seed-like beneath the soil, taking sustenance from it and growing in power, until he emerges fully-flowered.

Scale and archeological niceties aside, there is something similar in feel between fogous and the 'hollow hills' or *sitheans*, where the dead are buried and the faery make their homes.

Folk tale researcher Katharine Briggs tells us that in 15th century Britain, when healers and magicians wished to speak with the People of Peace, as the faery were called in Wales, one way was to bury a hazel wand "under some hill whereas you suppose fayries haunt" as a gift of appreciation for the healing or wisdom they might impart. [40]

James Walsh, 'the cunning man of Netherbury,' elaborated on the process when he was brought before the authorities in Exeter and asked how he spoke with faeries.

He replied that he did so:

Upon hyls, where as there is great heapes of earth, as namely in Dorsetshire. And betwene the houres of xii and one at noone, or at midnight. [41]

Sometimes the chosen were taken there, perhaps against their will, by the Earth spirits themselves, who recognised their potential as healers. In 1613, Isobel Halfdane of Perth claimed that she was carried half-asleep from her bed to a faery hill, where she remained for three days, learning the secret knowledge of spells and cures.[42]

There is also a tradition, common from northern Europe to North America, for people to be buried in the Earth as a form of shamanic healing or a type of vision quest, where they are able to resolve crises, seek clarity, and find their truths in nature. Like seeds, they also grow from the Earth and are reborn next day, free of the past and with the potential for positive change.

I have included burials like this in my plant spirit workshops and the results have been extraordinary. The group begins by 'digging their own graves' – although I am not keen on the word graves; it gives the wrong impression and evokes the wrong mood. I prefer the term 'seed beds' and those who dig them are gardeners of the soul.

There is a time for meditation and reflection after this, and then at sunset, the participants climb into their Earth beds and are covered, first with tarpaulin, and then with soil, so they can breathe, are comfortable, and can give themselves completely to the experience of healing and rebirth. They are 'uprooted' again next day at first light. Before that, though, something remarkable happens to these seedlings.

One student, Amanda, described her experience of a plant spirit workshop like this:

How to express what the experience meant to me... well last night I was laying on my bed with my 18-year-old daughter, who wanted to know all about what her Mum had been doing. I smiled at her and started to say something about it being a sort of retreat, and then something shifted inside of me, and probably for the first time ever, I really told her what was inside me... I cried and I laughed and I hugged myself with the sheer pleasure of some of the memories, insights and changes I held. She just sat there completely transfixed. It was the most honest conversation I had ever had with her... and to be honest it is probably the best example of what this experience has meant to me. I feel like when I speak with people, in fact in whatever I do, there is a real feeling of communion and honesty that floods through me and I wonder if I will ever be able to bullshit again! I feel this is a beginning of something profoundly real in my life and I am so deeply grateful for the experience, and only hope to do it justice.

It is not recommended that you attempt a ceremony like this alone and unsupervised, but if there is a cave nearby, some other entrance to the Earth, or a place "whereas you suppose fayries haunt", it would be fine and beneficial for you to go there "betwene the houres of xii and one at noone, or at midnight" (that is, at midday or midnight) and ask for healing, insights, or advice on your life and its direction.

Take a stick of hazel with you as a gift for the spirits and plant it in the Earth near where you sit. Remain there for at least six hours and watch the world around and within you for omens and signs which might provide answers for you or bring you the healing you need.

EXPLORATIONS: WAYS OF WORKING WITH PLANTS

Long ago, the truth to say
He has grown up and gone away
And it is but a child of air
That lingers in the garden there.
Robert Louis Stevenson, *Envoy For "A Child's Garden*
Of Verses"

Robert Louis Stevenson's poem, part of which is quoted above, laments the loss of childhood, when every garden is a magical place where we can "enter into other lands" to "kingdoms underground", and find "strange birds" which sing like the "bells on many fairy citadels".

In these lands, once, "other children used to play", but now they are all grown up and cannot hear us calling them, because their attention is taken by "play-business".

We can tempt them back to magic, though, these lost children within us, by creating a medicine garden of our own.

Growing fresh herbs and working the soil is a fine and obvious practice for any plant healer. And it need not be 'work' at all. Really, it is play.

When I first met Adam, his garden was the first thing that struck me. To me, a city boy, newly-arrived in the village, it was an untidy mess of weeds, herbs, and flowers growing wild with no apparent thought, planning, or care expended on it. As I grew wiser, though, it revealed its mysterious logic to me, for all of these plants were healers and arranged, not according to some modern artifice of straight lines and 'beauty', but with consideration for the plants which had an affinity for each other and liked to grow together.

That seemed like a strange philosophy to me, in those days of manicured lawns and ornamentation – and perhaps it still does to some. But gardeners and scientists nowadays are coming round to Adam's ideas and have discovered for themselves that the companion planting of different species together offers protection for both, since the predators of one plant are repelled by the other, and so tend to stay clear of all. Tomatoes love potatoes, for example, and basil will make sure that tomatoes stay pest-free. In other words, the plants take care of themselves; there is little work for us to do, except allow them to, and resist the temptation to interfere.

There is really nothing new in this idea. Medieval monks practiced companion planting in their herb gardens, with vegetables, herbs, and fruit grown in the same beds together, and with each used for both culinary and medicinal purposes.

As Henry Doubleday, of the Henry Doubleday Research Association, which researches and promotes organic gardening, once said: "The whole environment in which plants grow is much more than the sum of its individual parts, and all living things are inter-related and inter-dependant."

His words could have been spoken by Adam or a thousand different plant shamans.

Some herbs also attract insects beneficial to the whole garden by providing them with nectar and pollen, so these are always worth growing, even if you have no other healing uses for them. Examples are yarrow, dill, marigold, fennel, strawberry, sunflower, lovage, willow, golden rod, and thyme.

Other companion plants include:

Herb	Companion	The companion will protect the herb from	But is not compatible with
Allium (Onion family);	All vegetables and fruit trees;	Aphids, carrot flies, moles, and weevils;	Peas and beans; rue
basil	tomatoes	flies and mosquitoes	
Bay	Beans and grains	Weevils and moths	
Borage	Tomatoes and strawberries	Tomato worm	
Coriander	All vegetables	Aphids	
Chives	Carrots	Root flies	
Feverfew	Roses	Draws aphids away from other plants	
Garlic	Roses and raspberries	Aphids	
Hyssop	Cabbage	Cabbage white butterflies	Radishes
Marigolds	Most plants	Nematodes and aphids	
Mint	Cabbage and tomatoes	Butterflies, aphids, and flea beetles	
Pennyroyal	Roses	Flies, mosquitoes, and fleas	
Rosemary	Cabbage, beans, carrots, sage	Cabbage butterflies, bean beetle, and carrot fly. Growing a rosemary hedge around the outside of the garden will also protect some herbs, like oregano and thyme, from cold winds and driving rain	
Rue	Roses and raspberries	Beetles	Sweet basil
Sage	Rosemary, cabbage, carrots	Cabbage moth, carrot fly, flea beetle, and slugs	Cucumber
Tansy	Fruit trees, roses, raspberries	Flying insects, beetles, ants, and cucumber flies	
Thyme	Cabbage	Cabbage worm	
Yarrow	Planting close to aromatic herbs will increase their production of essential oils	Attracts hover flies, the larvae of which control aphids	

Another of Adam's 'innovations' was never to plant anything in a straight line. Rows of plants, he said, were unnatural and never found in the natural world. Again, this makes perfect sense. If you are a bug that loves lettuce – or fennel or marigolds – having them all laid out for you in a neat line means you can simply start at one end and munch your way through the lot. Having your preferred plants scattered throughout the garden, however, means you at least have to work for your supper.

The only real essential for herbs is that you plant them in a sunny spot since many of the ones we use today originated in the warmth and sunshine of the Mediterranean. Some are taller than others as well (such as bay, juniper, and angelica, which grows to over six feet), while some, like chamomile and thyme, grow at ground level, so you should take this into account when planning your garden layout, as you will probably not want taller herbs at the front of your sunniest borders.

There are various other subtleties to herb growing, but that is really all you need to know for now. Actually it is very simple and requires only one thing – a practice which shamans and plant doctors have been following for millennia: *observe nature and listen to its advice.*

What this means is that before you do any work to create a medicine garden, you sit with the land for a while and ask what *it* would like you to grow. Take a few walks in nature too and find places where herbs grow wild, then look for what plants grow with them. This is the Earth's natural order, which is to bring everything into a state of balance and co-operation. Planting ally herbs together in the same way means you are protecting and strengthening them by providing them with a natural ecosystem on your land.

The one thing that is often off-putting for would-be gardeners is the thought of all that digging. You don't actually need to dig a thing. Nature never does.

Instead, assuming you are starting with a patch of grass, simply apply a coat of mulch to it and cover the surface with a dark tarpaulin. You can then sit back and let the sun and the soil dig the garden for you. Your lawn will become fertiliser, which will also feed the soil. When the time for planting arrives, you don't even need to lift the tarp if you don't want to; just make holes in it and plant through it into the soil below.

That, apart from any obvious bits of garden maintenance and management, is more or less all you need do. Nature will take care of the rest.

Two thirds of people in the world today still depend on plants as their primary source of medicine, and our own ancestors relied on them too. By creating a medicine garden, you not only bring beauty and healing into your life, with the freshest herbs it is possible to get, you make a connection, through nature, to all the wise souls and healers in the world, now and in times past, who have worked with the magic of plants.

"All my hurts, my garden spade can heal," the poet, Ralph Waldo Emerson wrote, and that is never more true than in a medicine garden.

A society grows great when old men plant trees whose shade they know they shall never sit in.
Greek proverb

CHAPTER 6

HEALING THROUGH VISION: THE SACRED SOMA OF THE CELTS

The first time I saw him he was cooking mushrooms for himself
The next time he was asleep under a hedge, smiling to himself
Assuredly, some joy not quite of this steadfast earth lightens in those eyes
Swift as the eyes of a rabbit.
William Butler Yeats, *Fairy and Folk Tales of the Irish Peasantry*

Sometimes the need for healing, or for a healing vision of one's life, is so great that a special class of plants is employed by the shaman. These are teacher plants, plants of vision, or, as we know them in the West, entheogens: psychoactive plants which are used in a sacred context to invoke a spiritual or mystic experience.

The word *entheogen* was coined in 1979 by the ethnobotanists, Richard Evans Schultes and R Gordon Wasson, to describe these plants. The word means 'God within', and can be interpreted as 'that which causes us to become God-like'. In sin eating terms, they are 'plants of remembrance': allies which remind us of our origins as star-children and the many faces of God.

The word "within" should not be taken too literally, however. Certainly, teacher plants bring us face-to-face with our divinity and power, but their actions, unlike other plant allies, is to take us *out* of our selves, not further inwards, so our spirits are given wings. This is in contrast to non-psychoactive plants which, however we ingest them – in steam baths, sweathouses, as baths, perfumes, tinctures, or teas – bring their healing to us. Plants of vision are doorways, instead, and our guides for a journey of the soul into the universe itself, so we gain insights into its meaning and our place within it.

All cultures have their own teacher plants. In the Amazon, ayahuasca provides this sacred function. In the Andes, it is the san pedro cactus. In Haiti, it is wormwood; in Mexico, peyote. My book *Plant Spirit Shamanism: Traditional Techniques for Healing the Soul* has more about working with these South American plant teachers.

For the Celts, the magical plants of vision were, most likely, fly agaric (*Amanita muscaria*) – known as *Bia na Dé* in Gaelic – and, colloquially, as 'the faery stool' or 'magic mushroom.'

I say 'most likely' because the Celtic tradition is an oral one, and its magical and spiritual beliefs were not written down, except after the advent of Christianity, by monks we might suppose to have a vested interest in distorting the truth, if only a little, to make it fit their own beliefs.

To explore the possibility of entheogenic mushrooms as the sacrament of the Celts, therefore, we need to look for references to their spiritual powers in the folk and faery tales of Ireland and Wales, which are less likely to have received 'the hand of God' upon them.

Elizabeth Andrews, a 19th-century folklorist, made a study of these stories and summarised the general appearance of faeries in this way:

> Faeries are small people, but no mushroom could give them shelter. The colour red seems to be clearly associated with these little people.
> Fairies have red hair... and I have frequently been told of the small men in red jackets running about the forts. [43]

She also quotes another definition of the faeries, made by Yeats:

> Fairies are the lesser spiritual moods of the universal mind, wherein every mood is a soul and every thought is a body.

Elizabeth Andrews's first description may, indeed, refer subtly to fly agaric, a large mushroom with visionary powers which, fully grown, stands between two and eight inches tall, appearing, indeed, as "small people". They also have bright red caps: "red jackets" and "red hair".

If this is so, then fairies are not imaginary creatures, but manifestations of Yeats' "universal mind", which is allowed freedom of expression through the mushroom which refuses to "give them shelter" (ie. to keep these magical manifestations locked within the psyche) but liberates them as aids to our healing. Once freed ("running about the forts", as Andrews later remarks), very often the faeries bring us gifts of 'faery money', gold, good harvests, healthy cattle, or of healing and knowledge.

Similar hints are given in the folk beliefs and stories of the Welsh. In *British Goblins: Welsh Folk-lore, Fairy Mythology, Legends and Traditions*, Wirt Sikes records several of these. Concerning the origin of the *Tylwyth Teg* (faeries), he writes:

> There is a well-authenticated tradition of a race of beings who, in the middle of the sixteenth century, inhabited the Wood of the Great Dark Wood (*Coed y Dugoed Mawr*) in Merionethshire, and who were called the Red Fairies.
>
> They lived in dens in the ground, had fiery red hair and long strong arms, and stole sheep and cattle by night. There are cottages in Cemmaes parish, near the Wood of the Great Dark Wood, with scythes in the chimneys, which were put there to keep these terrible beings out.
>
> One Christmas Eve a valiant knight named Baron Owen headed a company of warriors who assailed the Red Fairies, and found them flesh and blood. The Baron hung a hundred of them...
>
> The beings in question were a band of outlaws, who might naturally find it to their interest to foster belief in their supernatural powers. [44]

In this description there are "Red Fairies" who lived "in the ground", had "fiery red hair" and stalk-like "long strong arms". Perhaps what the 'valiant knight' actually encountered on that

Christmas eve, therefore (whether he really slew "a hundred" of them or not, since all 'heroes' have a tendency to exaggerate) were the Druids of the Great Dark Wood, in communion with the spirit of the mushrooms.

If so, the story would be a victory for Christian over Pagan beliefs and a symbolic caution to Druids and other "terrible beings" not to meddle with the 'forces of darkness' in woods and mushrooms.

British Goblins also mentions the Welsh "Prophet Jones" – Edmund Jones, that is; a radical minister who was, for many years, pastor of the Protestant Dissenters at the Ebenezer Chapel, near Pontypool, where he was known for his "fervent piety and his large credulity with regard to fairies and all other goblins".

Jones held that the Bible alludes to faery rings, small circles of mushrooms where faeries are believed to congregate ("Matthew xii: 43: 'The fairies dance in circles in dry places'") and that they favour the oak tree "because of the superstitious use made of it beyond other trees in the days of the Druids".

William Jenkins, the schoolmaster at Trefethin church, in Monmouthshire, apparently witnessed faeries under an oak as well, and went to examine the ground around the tree. What he found was a "reddish circle wherein the fairies danced".

Thomas William Edmund, "an honest pious man" saw them too and heard the faeries talking "in a noisy, jabbering way; but no one could distinguish the words".

One documented effect of mushroom ingestion is glossolalia ('speaking in tongues'), and in mushroom ceremonies, such as those reported by Michael Harner in *Hallucinogens and Shamanism*[45], it is also common for the shaman to speak aloud about his flight to other worlds and the healing words of the spirits he encounters there, the role of the shaman being to act as interpreter, diviner, oracle, and intermediary for the spirits who bring us health and hope.

So, perhaps what Edmund heard was the voice of the faeries but spoken by and through the words of a Druid conducting a ceremony of healing like this.

The horse also plays an important role in Welsh faery tales. *British Goblins* tells us that, in Wales, the spirit of the horse "flits [and] The Welsh fairies seem very fond of going horseback".

This is interesting in itself, since flying horses (and reindeers) are common motifs in mushroom shamanism during the soul flight of the shaman to healing realms. The appearance and nature of some of these Welsh flying horses may be even more telling:

An old woman in the Vale of Neath told Mrs Williams, who told Thomas Keightley, that she had seen fairies to the number of hundreds, mounted on little white horses...

Another old woman asserted that her father had often seen the fairies riding in the air on little white horses; but he never saw them come to the ground.

'Little white horses' is a reasonable poetic description of *psilocybe* or 'magic' mushrooms. Also known as liberty caps, they are small, often white or yellow (ranging to lilac, brown, and purple), and grow freely in Wales. The description might also fit younger fly agaric, which emerge from the ground covered by a veil that encloses the entire mushroom, a fact that gave rise to legends of the magical 'serpent's egg' possessed by Druids. The gills and stem of fly agaric are also white, and the red cap is dotted with it too, remnants of the membrane which first encased it.

Another interesting claim from *British Goblins* is that Welsh sheep are the only animals that will eat the grass that grows in faery rings ("hence the superiority of Welsh mutton over any mutton in the wide world").

In fact, this is not true; sheep in Ireland (and perhaps all sheep) will eat them too. The Irish say that mushrooms walk across fields this way: by the sheep eating them and then dropping their spores in their excretia, providing them with a natural mulch in another part of the meadow.

The Prophet Jones apparently saw a flock of sheep who had eaten from a faery ring, when he was a young boy. The result was a "sheepfold of the fairies".

He was going with his aunt, early one morning, to his father's house at Pen-y-Llwyn, when he saw:

> The likeness of a sheepfold, with the door towards the south, and within the fold a company of many people. Some sitting down, and some going in, and coming out, bowing their heads as they passed under the branch over the door.
>
> I well remember the resemblance among them of a fair woman with *a high-crown hat and a red jacket*, who made a better appearance than the rest, and whom I think they seemed to honour. I still have a pretty clear idea of her white face and well-formed countenance. . .
>
> I wondered at my aunt, going before me, that she did not look towards them, and we going so near them. As for me, I was loth to speak until I passed them some way, and then told my aunt what I had seen, at which she wondered, and said I dreamed.

We know from the description of 'Prophet' Jones that he was a visionary (or less flatteringly, a man of "fervent piety and large credulity"), and children are in any case, more sensitive to spiritual phenomena and open to other worlds, so it is tempting to believe that what he sensed or saw were sheep surrounded, by the "red jacketed" and "white faced and well-formed" spirits of the plants they had ingested. Shamanic sheep! No wonder Welsh mutton is the best in the world!

THE IRISH SOMA

One author who has studied the myths and legends of the Celts in search of their healing sacrament is Peter Lamborn Wilson. It is likely, he says, that the first Celts arrived in Ireland from Siberia, where fly agaric is used as the sacrament in shamanic rituals, and that they brought this knowledge with them.

Others from Siberia migrated to India, and wrote of fly agaric in the Hindu *Rig Veda,* as Soma, a plant regarded as a god. Thus, Wilson refers to fly agaric as "Irish Soma" and contends that Irish and Indian settlers both learned about the visionary effects of these mushrooms from Siberian shamans in their country of origin. [46]

The legends of Ireland provide metaphoric references to the use of Soma. Those concerning Cú Chulaind, the warrior of Ulster, for example, portray him as having:

> Legendary moodswings: at one extreme, a battle-fury so intense that it terrified even his family, friends and fellow warriors; at the other, a torpor with vivid, prophetic dreams in which he languished for a year.

"It strikes me", says Thomas Riedlinger, writing on the fly-agaric motifs in the Irish myths of Cú Chulaind, "that aspects of both of these states, as described in the tales, resemble the effects of ingesting *Amanita muscaria*, the psychoactive mushroom with a bright red cap and white 'speckles', also known as the fly-agaric."

For a start, the description given of Cú Chulaind is that he has hair which is "brown at the base" and "blood-red in the middle," with "a crown of golden yellow", which is similar to the appearance of some fly agaric mushrooms. Then there are his moods and superhuman abilities. He is described as having a "salmon leap" – the ability to jump vast distances across land or high into the air – "warp spasms", "battle-fury", and "battle frenzy", always accompanied by a "hero's light" or halo around his head.

That the ingestion of fly agaric can bring great strength is attested to by various eyewitness accounts, such as this one from an 1809 paper on its usage and effects among the indigenous peoples of Siberia:

> The narcotic effect begins to manifest itself a half hour after eating... people who are slightly intoxicated feel extraordinarily light on their feet and are then exceedingly skillful in body movement and physical exercise. The nerves are highly stimulated, and in this state the slightest effort of will produces very powerful effects. Consequently, if one wishes to step over

a small stick or straw, he steps and jumps as though the obstacles were tree trunks" - which sounds much like the "salmon leap" of Cú Chulaind.

[Those who imbibe fly agaric] exert muscle efforts of which they would be completely incapable at other times; for example, they have carried heavy burdens with the greatest of ease, and eye-witnesses have confirmed to me the fact that a person in a state of fly-agaric ecstasy carried a 120-pound sack of flour a distance of 10 miles, although at any other time he would scarcely have been able to lift such a load easily.[47]

A few years ago, I was called as an expert witness in a criminal case involving trance and possession (in both the spiritual and legal senses of the word). The circumstances of the case are not important here, but so as not to leave you hanging, had to do with a man who had flown to the UK from Nigeria and was found to be carrying cocaine when he was stopped by Customs officials. His defence was that he had been entranced, or possibly drugged, by a group of men who had planted the cocaine on him before he boarded the plane.

What was interesting for me was that I got to have lunch with another expert witness, a toxicologist from one of the UK's leading teaching hospitals, who had an interest in mycology and planned to publish a book on the use of fly agaric in healing and warriorship practices. As a result of his studies, he had recently worked with a television company who had made a documentary with him to test one of his pet theories: that the Zulu War was fought by indigenous people under intoxication from the sacred mushroom. This had given them, not only superhuman strength and imperviousness to pain, but a sense of fearlessness and divine purpose in battle, much as they may have done for Cú Chulaind.

Whether his theory held water or not, the television company took it seriously enough to test it. Obviously, they couldn't stage another war, but what they could do was get two martial artists into a ring to fight it out for the cameras. In the first part of their experiment, the combatants met equally and fought a few rounds together. Neither emerged as a clear winner in this carefully matched contest. In the second part, one of the fighters was given five strips of fly agaric to consume. He was allowed to rest while it took effect, and then both fighters met again.

Except they didn't, exactly. According to the expert I was speaking to the fighter who had taken fly agaric simply flew across the ring as soon as the bell rang, hardly even touching the ground, and threw his opponent so hard that he ended up on the floor outside the ropes. He was not even breathing heavily when his opponent was counted out.

Similarities with Cú Chulaind's "battle frenzy" are obvious in this case, although in *Soma: Divine Mushroom of Immortality*, R Gordon Wasson is at pains to point out that "murderous ferocity… is conspicuously absent from our eye-witness accounts of fly-agaric eating in Siberia".[48]

While the capacity for superhuman strength may be present, then, it is not compelled to manifest, and the context in which the mushrooms are taken, as well as the intent behind their ingestion, is much more important. If they are eaten in a sacred environment, in ceremonies led by a skilled shaman, with full ritual precautions, and with a clear healing purpose, their gift, instead, is the ability to meet with the gods of blessings and well-being.

These healing powers may also be alluded to in the myths of Cú Chulaind. In the story of his "wasting sickness", the hero lies sleeping in what Fergus, another warrior, describes as "a vision".

This inspired dream leads him eventually to a green-cloaked woman who asks him to fight for the faery people of the *sídhe*. She then predicts his return to full health and strength, which comes to pass when he is told, in incantation, to: "Throw off sleep, the peace that follows drink" – to awaken, that is, from his Soma-induced visions.

Cú Chulaind's sleep is – more by luck than design, since he takes no special precautions – a visionary journey from illness, wasting, and soul-sickness, through an encounter with spirit powers, to a state of reinvigoration and well-being, as a result of "the peace that follows drink": the healing that arises from Soma.

More typically, a strict ritual must be observed in mushroom ingestion. According to Peter Lamborn Wilson, mushrooms are normally consumed in a set, or sets, of three: "The Rig Veda always speaks of Soma in sets of three cups and, in Siberia today, three Amanitas are still considered the proper ritual dose." [49]

An elaborate ceremony typically accompanies (or precedes) the consumption of Soma, which may take the form of a 'hunt' for the mushrooms, followed by the 'killing' of their spirit by symbolically attacking them with spears or arrows, so they are made safe for human consumption. They are then prepared in a way which is designed to honour their power and avoid their wrath.

Only then are they eaten, under highly contained, sacred conditions, and in a space defended by the shaman, who leads the ritual throughout.

Once ingested, the narcotic effects begin after about 30 minutes. Outwardly, the intoxication may appear as muscle spasms, followed by a sense of the fluidity of reality, and sensory disorientation. Inwardly, the shaman and those who partake of this sacrament are in communion with the gods.

The effects of fly agaric are easily transmitted to others, notably through their ingestion of urine from the first person to eat the mushrooms.

In fact, bizarrely, the ability of the mushroom to act in this way may be partly at the root of the Father Christmas rituals that are observed in the West. In the shamanic traditions of Siberia, from where Soma (according to Wilson) first originates, the shaman would ingest fly agaric in order to journey to the sky gods and bring back gifts of knowledge and power for his community. Dressed in a warm, fur-lined, ritual costume, with a thick belt hung with bells, the shaman would make his journey at nightfall to consult with these Otherworldly spirits. In the hours that followed, he would urinate and reindeers, enticed by the salt content, would eat the urine-covered snow and also become intoxicated.

'Flying' (intoxicated) reindeers with one sky-borne human (the shaman) who controls them. The similarities in costume. The bells and the belt. The red and white. The journey through the sky to deliver gifts. All the elements of the modern-day Father Christmas are there, creating an idealised version of fly agaric, which was often reflected in the Christmas cards of the 1930s and 40s, where Santa Claus is typically shown alongside a red and white mushroom.

Fly agaric also has a symbiotic relationship with the birch tree, the sacred tree of Siberia. Growing alongside it, it merges with the roots of the tree, helping it to absorb minerals in exchange for the sugars it offers. It is found wherever the birch is common, and grows freely in Wales, Scotland, other parts of Europe and the Americas, but less so in Ireland today because of the massive deforestation that has taken place in the last thousand years. For modern healers, however, that is not a problem, since possession of the mushroom is not prohibited by law and the internet means it can be easily purchased online.

Also of interest here is the role of the birch in the Welsh poem, *Cad Goddeu*, where it is a commander in the battle of the trees that the poem describes, and, according to Celtic scholar, Jean Markale, has responsibility for "transforming their withered aspect and bringing them back to life".[50]

In its healing and spiritual actions, this is also the principle effect of the fly agaric, the close companion of the birch, on human beings: to transform their illnesses and bring them back to life in all its fullness.

COMMUNION: THE CEREMONIAL USE OF MUSHROOMS

Fly agaric can be gathered for ritual from July onwards into the winter, but those found during the hottest months are said to be the most potent and passionate healers because they are then infused with the element of Fire.

The most powerful are said to dry themselves, ready to be picked for communion with man, and are considered stronger than those which are gathered early and dried artificially. Smaller mushrooms are also said to have greater power than larger ones, and their narcotic effects are more intense during the early growing phase.

They are best prepared for ceremonial use (according to shamanic tradition, as well as the advice of my toxicologist expert witness) by cutting them into thin strips which are boiled in milk for 30 minutes or so. The liquor is then drunk and the mushroom strips eaten. An alternative is to dry the mushrooms and add them to vodka, drinking the mixture when the liquid turns a shade of orange-red. Or they can simply be eaten.

The shaman and patient should both follow a diet or period of fasting before taking the plants. This has the dual effect of preparing the mind and soul for the ritual encounter, and ensuring that the stomach is empty, for faster absorption of the tea.

Fly agaric might also have been used in combination with sweating cures in the sweathouses of Ireland, and this may be another way of meeting its spirit: either by drinking mushroom tea before the sweat, or taking the Soma into the lodge where its intoxicating essence would be released by the heat and absorbed through the skin and breath, providing the patient with milder visions.

(The name fly agaric, by the way, has nothing to do with the powers of shamanic flight it offers, but, less romantically, because of its early use in Europe as an insecticide when sprinkled in milk it is still used like this in some parts of eastern Europe, such as Poland and Romania. The practice was first recorded some time before 1256, by the alchemist, Albertus Magnus, who wrote, in *De vegetabilibus*, fairly straighforwardly, that: "It is called the mushroom of flies, because crushed in milk it kills flies.")

The psilocybe (magic mushroom) is even more easily found and, in my experience of the Welsh tradition, is the preferred entheogen for healing and mystical experiences.

Magic mushrooms have a long history of use as a sacrament. They are depicted in rock paintings from the mesolithic period, and so-called mushroom stones (either natural or man-made) – such as those in the Irish Counties of Offaly, Galway, Clare, and Cork – still have ritual and spiritual significance in connection with ceremonial and/or mushroom use.

Similar stones can also be found in Wales. The historian, Sir

Richard Colt Hoar, wrote in his *Journal of a Tour in South Wales in 1793* of "a field between the town and the harbour (of Newport)", where he saw such a "druidical relict, resembling in some degree the one at Pentre Evan but infinitely smaller in its proportions. The upper stone resembles an umbrella or mushroom". [51]

Like fly agaric, the psilocybe experience is characterised by sensory effects, and by feelings of relaxation and bliss, where users may become lost in wonder and amazement at how even the most trivial of things – a word, a gesture, an image or a sound – contain great poetry and beauty.

Strange lights, halos, auras, objects that shimmer, sheen, ripple or breathe, may also become apparent, and sound may be experienced as divine in itself, or as a mood, feeling, taste, or colour.

It is as if all things are in some way alive, connected, and have a vast hidden depth to them – which, of course, they are and do, shamanically speaking, at least.

The mushrooms bring us closer to this truth and to our connection with all things as part of ourselves. A sense of melting into the environment or the air around, and of 'everything containing the seed of everything else' is also common as the user becomes one with this Oneness.

On the downside, such 'distortions of reality' can lead to an inability to distinguish 'fact' from 'fantasy', which is another reason why the shaman, as the guide who knows the spirit of the plants, must be present to support the patient or novice and help him understand the nature of his visions. He must also be a man of honour as well as a man of knowledge.

Possibly, this is alluded to in one of the Welsh stories of Pryderi, told in the epic tales of the *Mabinogion*. Pryderi was the owner of the only domesticated pigs – a sacred animal to the Celts. They were presented to him by the Underworld god, Arawn, but, in this tale, are stolen by Gwydion, who disguises himself to enter Pryderi's court, where he barters for the pigs, offering horses and dogs in exchange.

When the deal has been struck, however, and Gwydion has driven the pigs off towards Gwynedd, Pryderi discovers that the goods he has obtained through barter are, in fact, mushrooms, which promptly revert to their original form.

Gwydion, a wizard, knows the magic of mushrooms and, possibly, uses them to deceive Pryderi: a warning that the magician's power provides the intent for the mushroom experience, and that we should, therefore, choose our guides and our healers well.

Other common characteristics of mushroom healings are epiphanies and realisations about life, including the ability to deal with bad memories from a wider and more empowered perspective.

There have now been several scientific and medical studies of psilocybe which demonstrate their ability to act in this way and to impart highly beneficial effects to people suffering from emotional and mental (or spiritual) ill-health.

Their ability to cure problems such as depression and various forms of obsessive-compulsive disorder is also documented in medical studies where psylocybin has been administered and sufferers from both conditions have gone immediately into remission or experienced an "acute improvement in symptoms" which lasted for many months. This is in contrst to orthodox medication, which has limited benefits and some unwelcome side-effects. [52]

It was Timothy Leary who, inspired by the power of mushrooms, first began to explore their therapeutic benefits under his Harvard Psilocybin Project in 1960. His work demonstrated the inherant capability, quality, or spirit of plants to initiate a religious experience in his subjects and to bring them healing through greater self-awareness – and which, in 1963, got him sacked from Harvard University and hounded by the government as a consequence.

It is interesting, if not ironic, then, that in 2006, more than 40 years after Leary was fired for his experiments into the mystical and healing benefits of psilocybin, the US government funded its own study, this time conducted by John Hopkins University, into the spiritual effects of psilocybe mushrooms. How times change.

According to *HealthDay* reporter, E J Mundell, in this government-funded study: "Volunteers who tried the hallucino-genic ingredient in psychedelic mushrooms during a controlled study... had 'mystical' experiences, and many of them still felt unusually happy months later."

Which is exactly what Leary's research had already proved.

The John Hopkins study involved 36 adults who had never tried these mushrooms before. A third of the participants later said that their experience was the "single most spiritually significant of their lifetimes" and more than two-thirds reported it as among their top five most spiritually significant experiences. Two months after the study, 79% of the participants reported increased wellbeing or satisfaction; and their friends, relatives, and associates confirmed this.

The lead researcher, Professor Roland Griffiths, said that: "More than 60 percent of the volunteers reported effects of their psilocybin session that met the criteria for a 'full mystical experience' as measured by well-established psychological scales."

Most of them, he said, also became better, kinder, happier people in the weeks after the session. The researchers noted none of the 'permanent brain damage' and 'negative long-term effects' which are common in media scare-stories about magic mushroom and other teacher plants, and Griffiths added that "It's unfortunate that as a culture we so demonized these drugs that we stopped doing research on them."

Dr Herbert Kleber, former deputy director of the White House's own Office of National Drug Control Policy, under President George Bush, confirmed that there may be "therapeutic uses" for psilocybin, and was so impressed by the John Hopkins study that he wrote a commentary for it. "We know that there were brain changes that corresponded to a primary mystical experience," he said, but felt that as yet – scientifically speaking, at least – the results did not inform them "about the metaphysical question of the existence of a higher power". [53]

Since the existence of a 'higher power' and the experience of what this power might be are very personal things, this is not entirely surprising, and if this is the only criticism of the John Hopkins study, it is glowing praise indeed for psilocybin.

THE HEALING RITUAL

The proper sacred context, set and setting, for any encounter with teacher plants is crucial, so the patient is protected, supported, and guided in his encounter with the spirits.

The use of mushrooms by Mazatec shamans, for example, begins with purification and dieting, where the healer abstains from meat, eggs, alcohol, and sex for four days before the ceremony (*velada*) takes place. The ritual itself is always done in the dark, at night, in a sealed, sacred, space which no one may enter or leave until it is over.

Adam also recommended a period of fasting and quiet reflection, as well as bathing in herbal waters before an encounter with mushrooms, which he regarded as a doorway to the faery realms. Furthermore, in the Welsh tradition too, they should always be taken in sacred space, at night, and outside and in nature, since they are *of* nature, and it is nature which brings the healing.

In *Hallucinogens and Shamanism* Michael Harner describes the ritual process for mushroom consumption among the Mazatec; a process which is so similar to the procedures employed by Adam that it suggests a certain universality of understanding. This is not so surprising, either, since, as all shamans know, it is the spirit which is the real healer and the guide to the shaman in its needs and methods.

Firstly, according to Harner's observations, it is important to eat the mushrooms at night and in darkness, because: "The depths of the night are recognized as the time most conducive to visionary insights into the obscurities, the mysteries, the perplexities of existence."

Secondly, the ceremony must have the deliberate intent of providing healing and "therapeutic catharsis", for mushrooms are not just the "chemicals of transformation", but "the means given to men to know and to heal, to see and to say the truth...

> From the beginning, the problem is to discover what the sickness is the sick one is suffering from and prognosticate the remedy... The transformation of [the shaman's] everyday self is transcendental and gives her the power to move in the two relevant spheres of transcendence in order to achieve understanding: that of the other consciousness where the symptoms of illness can be discerned; and that of the divine, the source of the events in the world.

The patient himself may eat the mushrooms in search of this healing, but so too will the shaman, even if the patient does not. It is the job of the shaman to give voice to the patient's ailments, to interpret their messages, and, through this, to rid the patient of their intrusive spirits. "Together with visionary empathy, her principal means of realization is articulation, discourse, as if by saying she will say the answer and announce the truth."

The shaman, in this sense, is the intermediary for divine communications, whose job is "to enunciate and give meaning to the events and situations of existence". But it is the mushrooms which actually speak. "If you ask a shaman where his imagery comes from, he is likely to reply: *'I didn't say it, the mushrooms did'*."

This understanding of the spirit of these teacher plants is entirely consistent with the experience of people in cultures other than the Mazatec. Mark, a student who shared a mushroom ceremony with me in County Clare, Ireland, home of Biddy Early and the 'faery doctors', explains how their spirit spoke to him and the healing which subsequently took place:

> For years, I had been plagued with illness. Never anything serious, but always recurrent, or else a succession of minor problems, one after the other. It was probably seven years since I had been completely well. Illness had become something I was used to, and I had long lost track of any cause (if, indeed, there was one).
>
> The mushrooms opened a door for me into a new connection – not during the ceremony itself, but in the quiet time after-

wards, when I was alone, still, reflecting on my experiences, and ready to hear their message. It was then that my mind put two and two together – like one of those Aha! moments. I realised that I had stopped loving myself and that part of me *wanted* to be ill.

Seven years ago was when I had left my wife and son, and when my illness had first begun. I realised I'd been carrying a lot of guilt about leaving them, especially at losing so much time with my son, and I think my illness was my way of punishing myself.

If that was the case, it wasn't a rational response, because it was time for the marriage to end, but, at some *irrational* level, that was the start of my getting sick. Now, my mind – opened up by the mushrooms – had solved the problem for me in a way I could never had done if I'd just sat down and thought about it. In fact, I would have dismissed the idea that I'd created my own illness as laughable – if it ever dawned on me at all through normal thought. But, that night, I was clear that I had.

And the strange thing is, whether logical or not, I haven't been sick at all since then; not once in the last two years. I think I released a lot of guilt that night. I also understood that, to make amends to my son, I had to be well so we could do more together. So I *chose* to be well, and I have been. As a result of that decision, my relationship with my son has also improved.

Guilt, in sin eating terms, *is* also a sin: the sin of missing the mark and forgetting who we are; and, perhaps, of allowing self-pity (or, as Castaneda's don Juan, would say, self-importance) to consume us, instead of acting from the heart as a warrior.

Remembering ourselves and the powers that we have, and using them positively to atone for our sins if need be, and then do "the little things" – good in the world – is an expression of our truth and our love, and the start of genuine healing.

By opening our eyes, and taking responsibility for who we are, our souls are made whole once again.

EXPLORATIONS: HEALING THROUGH VISION

A process blows the moon into the sun,
Pulls down the shabby curtains of the skin;
And the heart gives up its dead
Dylan Thomas, *A Process in the Weather of the Heart*

Plants of healing and vision grow wild in the fields; we have only to identify them and to gather and use them respectfully for them to become our allies.

Because of the need for proper ritual and for the guidance of a shaman during the ceremonies that accompany their use, however, I am not going to particularly recommend that you experiment with them on your own, although it is, of course, your right and your choice to do so.

What I propose here, instead, is to commune with the *spirit* of the plant through more usual shamanic methods.

SPIRIT COMMUNION: THE SACRED WITHIN

Many of the compounds and neuro-transmitters that are present in plants of vision also occur naturally in the brain and can be enhanced through shamanic practices which restrict the amount of external stimuli we are exposed to.

Mushroom ceremonies always take place in darkness, for example, and darkness is one way to cut down on influences from outside ourselves so we can meet the sacred within. Another is to set your room to body temperature and lie naked (as we might in an Irish sweathouse), so you are more aware of the self within your skin, and to remain in silence.

When we do so, as Dr John Lilly found in his experiments with isolation tanks, a number of spiritual effects are produced, which may include spontaneous visions, shamanic journeys, and out-of-body experiences.[54]

Reducing stimulation and lying in silent darkness is therefore one route to ecstasy, which, with the proper intention, enables us to explore and gain a sense of the spirit and healing intentions of the plants we turn our attention to.

A possibility to enhance this process is to drink a tea made from the kava (*Piper methysticum*) plant, *methysticum* from the Greek for "intoxicating".[55]

Kava is, of course, no substitute for sacred mushrooms, and this is not why I mention it, but because it is known to bring its users a sense of calm, well-being, or euphoria; and, while it is not especially visionary, it can enhance the effectiveness of shamanic journeys and is an aid to clearer and more intuitive thinking. It is also quite legal.

The tea, also known as kava, is prepared by grinding the root to a pulp, adding a little water, and straining it. It is then consumed as quickly as possible. A moderately potent tea will take effect within thirty minutes and last for about two hours.

FAERY RINGS
Since it is the spirit of the plant that interests us in this work, an even simpler way to connect to the essence of mushrooms if you do not wish to or cannot injest them is to find a place in nature where they grow: a place of faery rings and sacred birch, and simply sit in silence with them one evening, making a quiet prayer that they provide you with the visions and healing you need.

There is an invocation for Grace and blessings in the *Carmina Gadelica* that seems appropriate for this, *A Charm for Night Shielding*:

> Thou Great God, grant me Thy light
> Thou Great God, grant me Thy grace
> Thou Great God, grant me Thy joy
> And let me be made pure in the well of Thy Health
> Lift Thou from me, O God, my anguish…
> And lighten my soul in the light of Thy love.

Whisper it to the trees and plants and then be still and open to what comes.

CHAPTER 7

PLANTS THAT LOVE US

When wind and winter harden
All the loveless land,
It will whisper of the garden,
You will understand.
Oscar Wilde, *To My Wife*

The Western medical view (and even the viewpoint of most herbalists and homeopaths) is that particular plants cure particular illnesses. In contrast, many shamans maintain that since all plants are gateways to nature, and nature is the gateway to the entire spiritual universe, essentially, *any* herb can treat *any* ailment, as long as the healer has a strong connection to its spirit and has enlisted the support of the plant through rituals and supplications.

My own experience so far, however, is that, while all plants love us and have an affinity for human beings at a soul-to-soul level, certain herbs *are* better healers for particular problems, just as some plant shamans (or herbalists or doctors) are.

In Wales and Ireland, folk healers and faery doctors had specialist skills in certain areas of healing, and earned their reputations based on their effectiveness in curing specific illnesses.

These cunning men and women did not advertise their services, and many still do not, but walk into a village pub in Wales or the West of Ireland and start chatting to one of the locals over a pint of Guinness and a Jameson, and chances are that the conversation may at some point turn to healing. Then, you might be informed about the talents of Mr O'Rourke or Ms Waugh, who "know how to cure the pneumonia and have skills with the lungs". Ask about arthritis or a broken arm, however, you will be directed to Mr Hughes and Miss Wood.

Animal welfare is a different matter, and "old Mr Murphy"

may be your answer here, because "he knows how to cure the pig".

All of these healers may live considerable distances from each other and from the patient, but it is still not unusual for people who need healing to make a pilgrimage of many miles (in the old days, on foot or on horseback) to consult the right healer for them. Any of them may be skilful in their own rights and capable of easing the discomforts of illness, but there are still experts to be found who know the 'way' of a particular malady and its cure better than others.

This stands to reason, since a familiarity with the disease brings a more intimate knowledge of its effects and the means by which they are alleviated. A healer who has cured himself of depression, or cancer or alcoholism, for example, and who has subsequently worked with others to cure them of the same problems, knows better than anyone what depression or cancer means, as well as the spiritual practices and herbs which can help.

Plants are like this too. Every plant knows how to heal, but some, because of their unique circumstances – where they grow; how they live; the community of other plants, animals and insects around them; the landscapes they occupy; the prevailing winds and weather they face – have an affinity for certain conditions and have learned to protect themselves against others.

These conditions affect us too, and the plants we should therefore choose as our allies are the ones that have grown strong and thrived in the same circumstances we face. By doing so, we not only benefit from their gifts of healing, but if we listen closely, we may also hear their advice for how we can change our lives so we become more balanced and healthy and do not have to get ill again.

In essence, their healing message is to become more plant-like ourselves, by finding a more harmonious way of being in the world. Author and herbalist, Eliot Cowan, makes a similar point in an interview on plant healing:

The way that a plant is in the world, the way it relates to the world and lives in the world... is its medicine.

A plant spirit medicine practitioner takes it upon herself to get to know plants, to make friends with them, to be informed by them. To recognize them, so that the plant feels free to share its medicine, its unique and beautiful way of being in the world with human people through the practitioner. So, in this way, the person can receive from Willow the capacity to bend and flex gracefully with the winds of change in their life, just as willows do.

In a similar way, each and every plant has its way of being, its medicine that it is willing to share with others if someone is willing to take the trouble to get to know it. [56]

As a result of our biology, socialisation, peer pressure, social roles, social expectations, and economic needs, men and women have different 'ways of being' in the world, just as plants do. While all plants heal, and many work just effectively for both sexes (although their healing actions may vary), there are some that are better suited to men or women, or which, we might say, have more of an affinity for men or for women. With that in mind, this chapter looks at some of the different healing needs of the two genders, and the plants that can help.

HERBS FOR MEN

The big issues in life (and our biggest taboos) concern matters of sex and death, both of which affect men just as much as they do women. Men go through puberty, experience hormone imbalances, react to life and social pressures, and undergo a form of menopause every bit as much as women.

It is strange and disappointing, therefore (as well as a dereliction of duty by the media) that while television schedules, and newsagents and bookstore shelves heave under the weight of self-help and complementary health titles for women, the comparatively miniscule amount of guidance available to men is almost exclusively focussed on articles about 'how to get better abs' or 'increase your penis size'. Men are worth more than this..

It is a real problem, for if men cannot find the information they need, and if the media does not take male health issues seriously enough to cover them, then men are being cheated of well-being and conditioned by the absence of information to believe that their health does not matter.

Just as serious is the lack of attention and funding given to men's problems by health authorities and governments which have the effect of excluding men from healthcare.

One example is the attention and financing given to the research and treatment of prostrate versus breast cancer. The latter we are all well aware of, while the former is hardly mentioned at all. Official figures show that women are 14% more likely to die from breast cancer than men are from prostrate cancer – a signif-icant, but not vast difference between the sexes. And yet, funding for breast cancer research is *660% greater* than that for prostate cancer research; a ratio of 47:1 in favour of women.

Why such a huge gap exists between men and women in healthcare provision and policy is a mystery. What it tells us though is that men need to do more to heal themselves by working with their allies in nature because the healthcare authorities are not taking their own responsibilities seriously in this regard.

One life change that is highly significant for men, but given little attention, is the male menopause.

Strictly speaking, of course, men can't experience menopause, since this is defined as the time when menstruation ends, but that doesn't mean that they don't undergo the same symptoms. Men go through a male equivalent to the menopause from the age of about 40 onwards, called andropause. It is hormone-related, and like its female equivalent, can lead to fatigue, depression, and loss of interest in life. Accompanying it, for many men, are feelings of powerlessness, low energy, and confusion. After a lifetime of activity, exertion, ambition, and the drive or pressure to compete and achieve (to 'get the girl', 'get the promotion', and 'get to the top'), now comes the realisation – accompanied by signs of aging, such as changes in body shape, loss of muscle tone, and greying or receding hair – that they have left their youths behind.

This can be frightening for men who now see their children

grown up and leaving home, and after all their years as care-givers and providers, are left wondering what they are for. Reflections on the past, regrets and melancholy can surface. Testosterone levels drop and oestrogen levels are confused, leading to anxiety and emotional disquiet which men tend to suppress, as they have been taught by society to do.

Thankfully, nature's medicine cabinet is stocked with herbs that can help with these physical and emotional changes.

Black cohosh is one plant that can assist us to reclaim our energy and passion for life. Its root, mixed with *saw palmetto berries, damiana, raspberry* and *chamomile*, makes an effective andropause-buster when equal parts are added to honey and hot water to create an energy-boosting tea. This can be drunk twice a day for up to three months. After that, take a month off the regime, beginning it again when and if you need to.

All of these herbs individually are also excellent healers. *Black cohosh* is used in many natural aphrodisiacs because of its reputation for dealing effectively with problems of male arousal and loss of libido. *Saw palmetto* berries are used to treat prostate problems and will tone the bladder, improve urinary flow, and reduce the frequency of urination.

Damiana heals the symptoms of depression, raises energy levels and is recommended as a pick-me-up, while *raspberry* balances the emotions and helps to regulate mood by cleansing the blood of excess hormones. It is also a tonic to the reproductive system and an excellent source of iron.

Chamomile calms anxiety, brings a sense of peace to the emotions, and is an aid to gentle sleep. Gardeners know it as 'the plant's physician' because it helps the growth and well-being of many other herbs, such as basil, oregano, and mint, by stimulating their production of essential oils when it is grown as a companion to them. It serves a similar function for us.

Four other herbs which are generally good for men at all stages of life, and especially for men after they reach their forties, are dandelion, red clover, ginseng, and apple.

Dandelion flowers, steeped in red wine, are often used as a tonic for the heart, and the sap of the plant is discutient, which means that it will help to disperse 'morbid matter'. This dispersal works on all levels, not just physical, but emotional, spiritual, and mental too, absorbing and dissolving negative thoughts and feelings as much as diseased tissues. Two cups of dandelion tea (each containing about three teaspoons of the herb) are taken daily. Similar amounts can be used for the other herbs in this section.

In Wales, dandelion roots are grated and mixed with the leaves, then eaten as a salad. In Worcestershire, dandelion flowers are used in an old recipe for dandelion wine, which makes an excellent tonic, and is good for the blood. It tastes quite pleasant, a little like sherry.

Dandelion wine is made by pouring a gallon of boiling water over a gallon of flowers, and letting it stand, covered with a blanket, for three days, stirring it from time to time. After this, it is strained, 3 ½ lbs (1 ½ kilos) of sugar are added, and the mixture is boiled for 30 minutes, along with the rind of an orange, a sliced lemon, and a little ginger.

When it is cold, yeast is added (usually on a piece of toast, which is floated in the brew), causing it to ferment. It is then covered again and left to stand for two days. Finally, the mixture is strained and decanted into a cask which is sealed and stored for two months. It can then be bottled or drunk.

Dandelion roots also make delicious coffee. They are cleaned and dried and then lightly roasted before grinding them for use. The grounds are almost indistinguishable from actual coffee, but much better for you.

Red clover is another herb which has healing potential for men. Called 'God-given clover' by some plant doctors and herbalists because of its many powers for well-being, it is rich in minerals, with calcium, magnesium, and vitamins B and C. In many countries it is used for the treatment of cancer, and also contains agents which help to thin the blood and prevent heart problems and strokes.

Ginseng will also lower the blood pressure and strengthen the heart and circulatory system, and is an excellent tonic for men in stressful jobs or with high-pressure lifestyles. Its effects are enhanced by combining it with vitamin E. It can be dieted by simply chewing a piece of the root, about the size of your fingernail, making it very easy to take.

Equally easy – and almost so commonplace that we miss their medicinal importance – are apples. They are among our finest healers and were regarded by the Celts as the fruits of wisdom and long life. In Scandinavian legends, they are the food of the gods, who ate them to renew their youth and vitality and ensure immortality.

Apples are rich in magnesium, potassium, vitamins C and B, and in oxygen-carrying atoms, which purify and cleanse the heart. In every 4 ounces (100 grams) of dried apples, there are two milligrams of iron and more phosphates than in any other vegetable or fruit.

Apples keep cholesterol levels down and the pectin they contain binds with cancer-causing compounds to speed their elimination from the body. An American study of patients undergoing chemotherapy showed that simple apple cider mixed with honey improved cancer recovery rates considerably. Those who were given the drink each day had *twice* the remission rate of those who received chemotherapy alone.

Care and attention to the prostate is important for men, and can help to prevent some of the problems that can accompany andropause. A natural, organic, low-fat, high-fibre diet will help to ensure a healthy prostate, and herbal boosters for the immune system can also help.

One of the best is *echinacea*, evidenced by its effectiveness in clinical trials for treating viral infections like colds through its ability to improve the functioning of the body's immune defences. Studies in America, published in *The Lancet Infectious Diseases*, found that echinacea reduced the incidence of colds by 65%, and taken with vitamin C, reduced it by 86%.[57]

Saw palmetto is also recommended for the prevention and treatments of prostate conditions. Other herbs especially recommended as helpful in cases of prostitis, a painful infection of the prostate gland, are yarrow, marshmallow, peppermint, ginger, and liquorice root. They also help to regulate the hormonal system, for increased libido and greater enjoyment of life.

HERBS FOR WOMEN

Women also face unique health issues as a result of their biology, including menstruation, pregnancy, and menopause, and there are herbs to help them at all stages of life's adventure. Two of the best herbs for women – and ones recommended even if no others are ever taken – are (as their names suggest) lady's mantle and motherwort.

Lady's mantle strengthens the reproductive system, regulates menstruation, and increases fertility. It has a special affinity for the breast and is often prescribed as a poultice for painful breasts or lumps in the tissue.

Its botanical name (*Alchemilla*) and its common name of lady's mantle both have mystical associations. The name of lady's mantle was given to it by the 16th century botanist, Jerome Bock (better known as Tragus) who named it after the Virgin Mary because of its miraculous powers. *Alchemilla* is derived from the Arabic word, *alkemelych* (alchemy), because of its ability to magically transform illnesses. Scottish plant healers believed that drops of dew held in the chaliced cup of its leaves were a healing elixir in their own right, and would also enhance the potency of any medicine they were added to.

Motherwort is another great healer, which calms premenstrual irritability and helps to restore emotional equilibrium by soothing the nerves. Perhaps this is what the herbalist Macer meant when he wrote that it acts against "wykked sperytis". Culpeper and Gerard are in agreement. Culpeper said of it that "There is no better herb to drive melancholy vapours from the heart, to strengthen it and make the mind cheerful, blithe and merry", and Gerard said that it cures "infirmities of the heart".

Motherwort is of benefit to women of all ages, from puberty to menopause. In younger women it will relieve the discomfort of menstrual cramps, regulate periods and bring on menstruation

when late, as well as providing a tonic for the uterus and reproductive organs. For menopausal women, it will balance the
hormones, cool hot flushes, and moderate mood swings to lift
depression.

Nettle, rich in minerals, iron, calcium, and vitamins, is a
powerful ally for pregnant women. It can also help to stop
bleeding after childbirth and is nourishing for nursing mothers. It
also has health-giving properties for foetuses and newborns,
helping to build healthy bones and tissue, and improving the
quality and quantity of breast milk.

Angelica – the Herb of Angels or Root of the Holy Ghost – is
another female herb. According to legend, it was revealed in a
dream by an angel as having the ability to cure ills and protect
against evil spirits, enchantments, and witchcraft, hence its name.
It is rich in antioxidants and has a strengthening effect on the
endocrine system. It will also help balance the hormones.

The following five herbs have also been recommended to men,
but for different reasons, proving, as the plant shamans say, that
the same herb can be used for many applications because it is the
spirit which heals through its intelligent awareness of each
patient's needs. These herbs are ginseng, chamomile, dandelion,
red clover, and raspberry.

Ginseng root is rich in nutrients and aids the balanced
production of oestrogen and progesterone, making it effective for
the relief of premenstrual and menopausal symptoms (it should
not, however, be used when pregnant).

Chamomile will calm the nerves and is often prescribed for
hormonal problems with an emotional content. Chamomile and
ginseng make an excellent combination as a tea.

German chamomile is, as its botanical name (*Matricaria*) and its
more common name, mother herb, suggest, used for gynaeco-
logical conditions. In maternity wards in Germany it is given to
nursing mothers and their babies.

Red raspberry leaves are rich in calcium, and are well-known for
their ability to strengthen and tone the uterus during pregnancy,
preparing it for childbirth. Raspberry leaf tea helps to relieve

morning sickness, and provides some relief for labour pains. The leaves feed the nervous system and are also an excellent fertility herb if you are trying for a baby.

Dandelion roots may be used by women as a poultice to help with painful breasts. They can also be used as a douche, along with calendula, marshmallow and yarrow, or in a sitz bath, to inhibit the growth of Candida and help prevent yeast infections.

To make the bath, prepare a tub of warm water and add a few drops of tea tree oil and an infusion of dandelion, along with three tablespoons of natural yogurt for each quart of water. Sit in this twice a day, and avoid sex until the infection has gone.

Red clover is often the herb of choice when treating more serious breast and reproductive problems, such as ovarian cancer. The effected area is massaged with an infusion of the herb in warm oil, or a poultice can be placed over it. It can also be drunk as a tea – up to four cups a day – for the same conditions.

ILLNESS AS A METAPHOR

Despite the differences in male and female biology, however, illnesses in general – or rather, the root processes that give rise to illness – are the same for both sexes and for people of all ages.

The term *'Illness as Metaphor'* was invented by the social commentator Susan Sontag during her experience of breast cancer. In her book of that name, she explores the idea that the nature of any illness is connected to the nature or personality of the sufferer: that they have qualities in common and an affinity for each other in some way; "that the disease expresses the character" or "the character causes the disease – because it has not expressed itself."[58]

Illness, that is, is something we are not saying, an energy we are not releasing, or a form of dis-ease we are not letting go of, and which must therefore find some other way of expressing itself.

Our illness *is* its expression, which takes a form that is most consistent with our own make-up (colds for 'cold' or emotionally reserved people; fevers for those who are 'hot-tempered' or holding in anger, etc), and, in every case, it has a message for us.

This message, at its most fundamental, is that we are energetically or emotionally blocked in some way and have lost our sense of engagement with life; that we do not love ourselves; or that we feel guilt, shame, or disappointment about who we are or what we have become. Then as Sontag says, our "Passion moves inward, striking and blighting the deepest cellular recesses".

The feeling of a passionless soul is evoked in the poem, *Weariness*, by George Russell ('A. E.'):

Where are now the dreams divine
Fires that lit the dawning soul...

Mother, all the dreams are fled
From the tired child at thy feet.

These ideas are similar to the sin eater's view of illness: that when love – and more especially, self-love – leaves, we make ourselves available to ill-health.

The way that illness is then expressed is characteristic of who we are and what we have lost, just as it was for the patient I described earlier, who was suffering from hypertension (high blood pressure) – a disease that affected his heart – because, at the level of his soul, he knew that his heart was broken.

The form of our illness therefore contains the seeds of our healing by showing us who we are and how we need to change so we can find in ourselves once more the love that we have lost.

These ancient ideas, of illness as a symbolic message, have recently been given credence by new findings in psychology and neurology.

Psychoneuroimmunology, a term coined by Robert Ader of the University of Rochester, is a new field of mind-body research that studies interactions between an individual's thoughts, feelings, and behaviour, and the workings of the brain, endocrine, and immune systems.

Following Ader's work, we now know that physical illnesses do not – and never did – arise from purely physical causes, but from 'invisible' sources, which may at first seem totally unconnected to the illness itself.

Stress is one invisible cause of illness, for example, in the sense that it does not exist objectively in the world, but depends on our perceptions of it and the way we respond to it. Thus, two different people in the same situation might view their circumstances very differently; one thriving on them and the other becoming ill.

If we enjoy stress, we might never have a problem, but if we are the sort of person who does not respond so well to it, the effects can be severe. One study found that events such as divorce, bereavement, and unemployment affect the immune system and decrease the numbers of T-cells, whose job it is to destroy infection. Without these cells to help us, heart disease and cancer can be some of the outcomes. But these conditions are not the illness, per se; they are merely the symptoms of dis-ease, which is our experience of the life events that caused our immune systems to become depressed.

What really harms us is soul sickness arising from the choices we make of the ways we engage with life. The symptoms of illness are the visible signs; the messages from our souls that we need to make new choices.

Research tells us that anxiety, fear, anger, uncertainty, guilt, grief, feelings of aloneness, and lack of love are the real problems we face, and that these can give rise to real and physical symptoms.

The immune systems of those who care for Alzheimer's sufferers, for example, and who feel isolated and alone, have been found to be compromised for up to two years after their caring ends.

Wounds take longer to heal and are more prone to infection among those who are under pressure at work, or in their relation-ships with their families.

Divorce and depression go hand-in-hand, and both lead to reduced T-cell levels and an immune system which is depleted of the energy and resources it needs to fight off infections.

All of these outcomes arise from our decisions – to be alone, to work long hours, to manage our relationships in a particular way.

Getting better therefore begins with new choices.

The sin eater's approach to confession is a way of helping patients to examine their choices and look at dis-ease in a more rounded and inclusive way.

The shaman knows that even when a patient appears *physically* healthy, if she *feels* unwell, she has an illness. If that sounds strange – the idea that someone who is physically OK can still be ill – consider hypochondria: the belief that you are unwell when you are not.

Firstly, while there may be no physical symptoms, the *belief* that you are suffering can itself cause psychological and emotional discomfort, and the stress these feelings produce can also lead to physical illness, like a cycle completing itself.

Secondly, from the viewpoint of the shaman, hypochondria *is* the disease, and he must therefore look for the message it holds: why, that is, the patient believes herself to be unwell or, perhaps, why she feels she *deserves* to be ill.

This is a welcome contrast to the orthodox medical model, where, if an examination cannot find a physical or organic problem, the illness itself is often dismissed as psychosomatic or resulting from factors such as anxiety, depression, or guilt, which are deemed unimportant.

These 'unimportant' factors, however, are the very ones which lead to chronic physical illnesses if their subtle messages are not heard and the spirit of dis-ease begins to raise the volume of its communications.

It has been suggested that two-thirds of all diseases have a psychological or psychosomatic cause. The shaman calls them soul sickness, and they are real.

The Welsh poet, Dylan Thomas, wrote that:

Love and his patients roar on a chain;
From every tune or crater
Carrying cloud.
Dylan Thomas, *On a Wedding Anniversary*

Love, or the lack of it; self-love and our rejection of it, are the causes of suffering. It is what makes us "roar on a chain, carrying cloud". To be whole, healthy, and happy, it is our capacity for love that we must develop.

There are herbs that can help:

Sage – sometimes referred to as *S. salvatrix* ('sage the saviour') – has long been used by Breton Celts to soothe grief and to bring wisdom and a new sense of perspective through which greater love is possible.

A Welsh folk cure for ague is also provided by sage. Ague (or *aigue* as it was then written) is a word from the Middle French, which entered English in the 14th century. It has the same origin as acute, which is derived from the Latin *acutus*, meaning sharp or pointed. A *fievre aigue* is a 'sharp or pointed fever', characterised by chills and sweating, often with no physical cause, much like an anxiety or panic reaction.

The cure was to chew sage leaves while fasting and making prayers for healing, and then spit them out so that the sickness of the soul would be carried away with them. This was repeated for nine consecutive mornings, after which the illness would be gone. A less dramatic alternative is to boil the leaves in vinegar and drink it as a tonic.

Tarragon is another of the herbs of love. The name is a corruption of the French word, *Esdragon*, which is derived from the Latin *Dracunculus*: Little Dragon.

According to Christine Scallan, in *Herbal Cures: Healing Remedies from Ireland:* "Like all herbs which have the word 'dragon' in their names, it was believed to contain the antidote to all manner of venomous bites and stings." [59]

'Venomous bites and stings' are often at the root of our feelings of inadequacy or lack of worth or of our problems with love, and tarragon can help us to quieten these and find comfort in who we are. According to the 17th century diarist, John Evelyn, "'Tis highly cordial and friend to the head and heart". It can be drunk as a tea or, again, prepared as a tonic vinegar.

Our best medicine, however, is to rekindle our feelings of love, excitement, and passion at the world, and the greatest healer of all is nature, which helps us to reconnect with the source from which we came, and find our peace and stillness.

In that quiet place of the mind, the seeds of love might be sewn.

EXPLORATIONS: PLANTS THAT LOVE US

The power is ours to make or mar
Our fate as on the earliest morn,
The Darkness and the Radiance are
Creatures within the spirit born.
George William Russell ('A. E.'), *The Twilight of Earth*

ILLNESS AS A METAPHOR

In exploring illness as a message or metaphor for the things in our lives which do not serve us, there are four principles to consider:

1. That illness is the manifestation of a stuck energy which tells us that we are out of flow with love, or that the life we are leading and the choices we are making are not healthy ones for our souls.
2. That illness will manifest to tell us this in a way which is characteristic of us so that it carries the resonance of our souls and appears in a form that we are most likely to notice and pay attention to.
3. That there are particular herbs which – by virtue of where they grow, or the conditions they live under – have faced a version of the same life challenges as us, and on a symbolic or metaphorical level, have found *their* solutions to *our* problems.
4. That, by understanding the real message of our illness, rather than its physical symptoms, we can make better life choices and, as part of our healing, work with the plants aid our return to health.

Our solutions, therefore, require us to take responsibility for our illnesses, since it is *our* souls which are manifesting them to tell us that something is wrong. It also requires our willingness to change, and our choice to do so.

This is not always as easy as it seems. The medical intuitive Caroline Myss, in her book *Why People Don't Heal and How They*

Can, speaks about how we can choose to stay sick if we wish, since ill-health sometimes brings benefits of its own.

> One day, in passing, I introduced a friend of mine to two gentlemen I was talking with. Within two minutes, my friend managed to let these men know that she was an incest survivor. Her admission had nothing whatsoever to do with the conversation we'd been having, and in a flash I realized that she was using her wounds as leverage. She had gotten to the point that she defined herself by a negative experience...
>
> I saw that, rather than working to get beyond their wounds, people were using them as social currency... They were confusing the therapeutic value of self-expression with permission to manipulate others with their wounds. Who would want to leave that behind?
>
> We are given a finite amount of energy to run our physical bodies, our minds, and our emotions, as well as to manage our external environments. When we choose to siphon off some of this energy to keep negative events in our histories alive, we are robbing that energy from our cell tissue, making ourselves vulnerable to the development of disease.

If we are ready to change and be well, however, illness can be a profound transformational experience and bring great blessings into our lives.

To explore this, think back to any illness you have had. What, at a symbolical level, might it have meant? Could it be, for example (and to take a seemingly trivial example), that your runny nose and the cold you had last January was a way for your body to release Water – the element of the emotions, which, when out of place in the body, can mean sadness, loneliness, or grief? What else was happening in your life at the time that might suggest this?

Reflect on this for a while in relation to your illness and see what connections you can make. Sum up your illness is one or two words if you can – not as a symptom (its physical presence) but as a soul-message. For example, in this case 'cold' equals 'feeling alone'.

Incidentally, in the research now being conducted by psychologists, isolation and depression leads to a suppression of our immune responses, which very often does manifest as a cold or flu. Symbolically, we might say, we *get* colds when we *feel* cold.

It would be possible, however, for a suppressed immune system to manifest illness in other ways than this, since illness arises in a way that is characteristic of us. A person who has a 'weak heart' as a consequence of his feelings of aloneness might manifest dis-ease in a quite different way, but the root of the problem is the same.

What, then, is the message your soul is giving you? What does the nature of your illness say about the person you are and the way you live? And, knowing this, what new choices can you make for your healing and to avoid a recurrence of the problem?

The herbs which can help with this are not necessarily the ones which might be recommended by a doctor who is focussed on the symptoms of the illness, but ones which comfort your soul and bring you warmth and peace; which, ultimately, bring you love.

For a cold arising from loneliness, for example, a sin eater or Shaman might choose mint and soothing honey instead of the antibiotics or echinacea recommended by a doctor or herbalist, because mint is one of the most gregarious of herbs. It grows like wild *fire* in opposition to cold, and has conquered any desire for aloneness within itself.

Knowing the message of your soul, what herbs suggest themselves to you as a tonic to prevent the illnesses you may be prone to?

Close your eyes and journey if you need to, until an appropriate herb suggests itself; one that just 'feels right' to you. Then conduct a little research to see what else you can discover. If everything checks out and makes sense to you, diet that plant for a while to see if it helps and what effects it has.

It is these wider messages from our souls that we must hear: the ones telling us that we must get back in flow with love, feed and nourish our spirits, and make wise choices in our lives so that we can be well.

Reflect on this for a while, and see what you can discover about yourself.

WAYS OF WORKING WITH HERBS

For simplicity in the previous chapters, we have concentrated mainly on teas and infusions as a means of dieting health-giving herbs and rediscovering our radiance.

There are many other ways to prepare plants as herbal medicines, however, and to be a well-rounded plant doctor, it is useful to know some of these.

This section is to encourage you to practice your skills by preparing herbal cures in a number of different forms. These are just the mechanics of herbal preparation, however, and to be a *shamanic* plant healer, you will, of course, also follow appropriate procedures and rituals in the hunting and gathering of plants, and in your relationship to them, before and during your preparation of them in these ways.

Compresses: To make a compress, soak a length of lint or gauze in an infusion or decoction of the herb (see below) and bandage it to the skin, either warm or cold.

Decoctions: Soak the herbs in cold water for 30 minutes or so (a ratio of one tablespoon of dried herbs to two pints of water is normally used), then bring them gently to the boil and simmer for twenty minutes. The decoction is then ready. Decoctions are usually applied externally (as a compress), but they can also be drunk or used in floral baths.

Infusions: Teas, infusions, and tisanes are one and the same thing. They are made by pouring approximately ½ pint of hot water over a teaspoon of the dried herb, or two teaspoons of fresh herb. The normal dose is one or two cups a day.

Oils: Add fresh herbs to a jar of sunflower oil and cover the top with muslin for two weeks and allow the herbs to steep, shaking the jar each day. Then strain out the herbs and bottle the liquid.

Ointments and creams: Add one ounce of beeswax or lanolin to four fluid ounces of herbal oil (see above) and simmer the mixture gently in a saucepan on a low heat for ten minutes, stirring constantly. Strain the fluid while still warm into a clean container and apply the lid when it has cooled.

Poultices: Poultices are made by sandwiching warm herbal ointment (see above) between two layers of muslin, and applying the bandage to the skin until it cools. Repeat this as necessary.

Syrups: Three tablespoons of honey are added to ½ pint of herbal infusion (see above) and brought slowly to the boil in a saucepan until it thickens. Let it cool then pour it into a clean glass bottle.

Tinctures: These are made by placing herbs into a bottle and adding alcohol (usually vodka or brandy, but rum or whisky is sometimes used). This is left to steep for nine days (or longer for a stronger taste), then strained and decanted into a new bottle. The usual ratio is one part of the crushed fresh herb to five parts of alcohol. A little water may also be added to dilute the alcohol if you prefer.

CHAPTER 8

RETURNING THE LOVE OF THE PLANTS

I saw eternity the other night
Like a great ring of pure and endless light.
Henry Vaughan, *The World*

It is interesting to reflect that, in a way, we are all descended from plant healers and faery doctors, since our ancestors – not all that long ago – relied on plants for their medicines, food, clothing, building materials, and for many other uses.

This was before the days of modern medicine, and we should bear that in mind: that medical science does not have the only answers. Furthermore, the answers it does have (in fact, its entire existence), it owes to people like our grandfathers and grandmothers, whose cures have been taken, adapted, and repackaged by modern medicine to create brand new 'wonder drugs', which are really just plants in disguise.

If we are still for a moment, we can probably all think back to a few of the cures or observations from nature that our grandparents or parents have taught us, which turn out to have validity.

"Red sky at night, shepherd's delight" is an old saying in England. It means that if there is a red glow to the evening sky, the morning will be fair, and it's true.

"An apple a day keeps the doctor away" is another, and what we now know of the healing power of apples could fill a book. I hardly began to list their qualities in the last chapter.

There is a poem from 18th century Wales, called *Baled yr Hen ?r o'r Coed*, which suggests how folk cures and traditonal healing has been always been passed on – from mouth to ear and heart to heart.

Gan fy nhad mi glywais chwedel

A chan ei daid y clywsai yntau
Ac ar ei ôl mi gofiais innau

I heard my father tell a tale
He heard it from his grandfather
And I remembered it from him.

It hints at the wisdom that may be locked away in the subtle (sometimes oblique) folklore of our ancestors about the powers of the plants. In following these hints, we involve ourselves in a great adventure, because we become plant detectives, guided by the words of old souls.

Like this song, folk healing has depths to it, slowly unravelling its mysteries as our knowledge and experience grows.

Its title, *Baled yr Hen ?r o'r Coed,* means *The Ballad of the Old Man of the Woods,* suggesting the importance of nature, the dark woods, and the trees in the lives and learning of our ancestors.

The title becomes even more interesting to plant detectives, however, when we discover that Old Man of the Woods is the name of a mushroom.

Our Celtic ancestors left us clues to their ways of healing and to the spirit of the plants (see the chapter on teacher plants), sometimes deliberately to protect their wisdom from outsiders, and sometimes because knowledge must be worked for.

I decided to do a little research on the Old Man of the Woods. I found almost nothing, but what I did learn about *strobilomyces,* its botanical name, is that it is not an attractive mushroom. It is black, scaly, brooding, almost diseased-looking. That, and the fact that it tends to grow alone in isolated places and dark coves, means it has been mostly overlooked. It is not even used as a food source, although it can be eaten. But of its healing applications, there was nothing.

I can be tenacious, though, so I found an image of *strobilomyces,* tuned into it, as I've been suggesting you do in this book, then closed my eyes and took a journey to its spirit.

"What are you for?" I asked.

Almost immediately it shot back an answer, as if it wanted to talk and had been deprived of company for too long, as old men can sometimes be.

"Cancer," it said.

Looking at the outward appearance of the mushroom, misshapen and black, that answer now seemed obvious, and it is true, of course, that old men often do succumb to cancer. So I googled it: 'strobilomyces' and 'cancer'. There was not much, but there was just enough to show that the Old Man of the Woods is now being taken seriously in cancer research. [60]

I wouldn't mind betting that the way in which strobilomyces grows, alone and in isolated places, and its apparent loneliness and keenness to talk, means it might have other uses too, in depression or in helping us to overcome shyness and anxiety in social situations, but I'll leave that research for you. As for the Old Man of the Woods and its uses in cancer, time will tell.

This is how our knowledge of healing grows: by trusting our ancestors, who trusted the plants, and listening to the messages of both, even if they are given to us in faery tales, myths, legends, and scattered hints and fragments in songs about old men and mushrooms.

Sean O' Suilleabhain, the head of the folklore department at University College Dublin, has a certain passion about him when he writes of the sheer number of discoveries like these, and all of the modern medical cures that would not have existed without the insights of our ancestors: the plant healers of the past.

His list goes on, but he knows he's only scratching the surface, and that modern medicine owes all that it is to these pioneering men and women, the cunning folk who knew the soul of men and the spirit of plants, and who, through their explorations and endeavours, learned their healing methods.

African medicine-men have for a long time used the bark of a certain type of willow to cure rheumatism with salicyl; the Hottentots knew of aspirin; the natives of the Amazon River basin used cocillana as an effective cough-mixture, and curare, which they applied to arrow-tips to stun their enemies, is now used as an anaesthetic.

The Incas have left us cocaine; ephedrine reached the Western world from China; cascara was known to the North American Indians.

From the juice of the foxglove was derived digitalin for heart-ailments; and finally, here in Ireland, moulds from which penicillin has been derived were traditionally used for septic wounds. [61]

We have a lot to thank the faery doctors and plant healers for. And yet, Patrick Logan, the author of *Irish Folk Medicine*, tells us that, in Ireland these days:

> In order to learn about the treatments used it is necessary to ask elderly men... few young men... know anything about them. As for veterinary folk medicine, he says, it is "almost forgotten".

It is the same story in Wales. In his introduction to *Welsh Folk Customs*, Trefor M Owen, curator of the National Museum of Wales, asks:

> Looking back from our own day at the period in which folk customs flourished, how are we to account for their decay and disappearance?
> Why have folk customs which have had such a long life finally vanished? They were often archaic, even when they were actively carried on, why then should they have died? [62]

In answer, he says, firstly that the old communities which refined these healing practices and relied on these customs, have long since ceased to exist. "No longer are the countryside communities the intimate little worlds they were in the last century." The railway and the motor car, and, these days, television and internet culture, have changed our relationships to nature and the places where we live.

Communities have broken down, the pace of life is faster, and we now have a huge amount of technology at our disposal, which makes its demands on us too. All of these things have become more seductive to us than the natural world or the quality of our relationships with it and with ourselves.

Owen wrote in the 1950s about the historic decline of plant spirit wisdom and folk healing that:

> The vitality of peasant life, turning inwards upon itself and creating in the natural course of things a surplus of social life from its very intimacy and closeness, was sapped by the ever-increasing mesh of social relationships.
>
> No longer would any custom that had lost its *rationale* continue to exist merely as a manifestation of the intimate and intense life.

This is ever-more true today.

Secondly, Owen points to the rise in Wales of the Methodist Movement, which frowned upon folk healing and natural cures as 'the Devil's work'. In Ireland the Catholics and Protestants developed a similar distaste for the healings of Biddy Early and the other faery doctors, and petitioned for their trial as witches. In any case, what Owen is referring to is the growth in the power and influence of mainstream religions to the detriment of traditional spiritual practices.

> The religious reformers in their zeal attacked both harmful and harmless customs indiscriminately. Their attitude was that idle pastimes, however innocent they might appear, distracted men from their main task of searching their souls and cultivating their spiritual life in order to work out their salvation.[62]

However misguided the views of these zealots may have been towards plant healers, since these men and women were essentially working for the same ends as the zealots themselves: to help their patients find answers in their souls to the questions of existence which bothered them, and to cultivate the spirit in their lives, the words of these Ministers had clout. Anything that stood in their way was condemned as "foolish and sinful".

And yet, when we consider the many blessings that plant healing has brought us, including the various cures that Sean O' Suilleabhain lists, it seems that there must be something more at the root of its decline. For, even a practice which really was foolish and sinful would surely have continued and been accepted because of its many positive outcomes.

There must have been some other factor at play, and I think the answer is a simple one: we have fallen out of love with nature.

For the last two or three hundred years – coinciding with the beginning of the end for folk healing – we have been cutting down trees at an unprecedented rate to fuel our industries and, nowadays, our fast-technology and fast-food lifestyles. We have been polluting our rivers and seas and pumping greenhouses gases into the atmosphere with little concern for the consequences. We have forgotten our sacred promise to the elements and the part that we really play in nature.

There are not many of us who would poison those we love like this, for example. So, perhaps we have fallen out of love with ourselves too, because the consequences of our actions are real enough and they affect us all, as the climate crisis makes plain. And yet many people still refuse to do anything about it, even if only to take care of themselves.

Stepping outside of nature may have given us the illusion of invincibility and blinded us to the inconvenient truth, but even if we have no love for the natural world these days, if we even loved ourselves, surely things would be different.

It was not always this way. In the Bunratty museum in Ireland, there is a lovely example of byre cottage from County Mayo, where people and their milking cows once lived together. The bedrooms are on one side, the cattle area on the other, and the space in the middle was for both.

In Dingle, there are houses where the hearth fire was shared by the family and their pig, which, as a sacred animal to the Celts, was welcomed into the home. Keeping them outside would be like expecting a family member to live in a sty.

I am not quite so foolish as to suggest a return to such practices now (although I have a great fondness for the pig), but perhaps it is not too late for us to "do the little things", as Saint David encouraged us to, so we feel ourselves a part of nature once again.

Doing the little things is not an onerous task. Mostly it requires that we slow down to the pace of the nature, notice it, and unplug ourselves from the computers, TVs, iPods, and other machines that we have allowed ourselves to become the servants of, so that, once in a while, we can share the adventure of opening our minds to new possibilities. Any of the following would be a start.

Lose yourself in the woods from time to time. We live such sheltered lives, enclosed and contained in our suburban landscapes, that we forget what it is to be part of a living planet which is worthy of our respect and worth saving. We need to rekindle our love for nature and for a full and meaningful life, so that they become important to us once more. All that really means is that we take time for nature and for ourselves to feel human again.

Honour your need for community. Human beings are social animals. We are co-operative at heart and we need others around us to share our joys and sorrows and to give us perspective on life. Alone in the boxes we call homes, we involve ourselves less and less in community living and community spirit these days. Many of us do not even know our neighbours' names. Think about what you might do to develop a greater sense of community where you live, so that you engage with the world more fully.

It is by peaceful co-operation at a local level that positive change is possible. A world revolution starts simply: by shaking hands across a garden wall.

Don't be persuaded. Think about your values, about what's important, and what moves you, before you succumb too readily to someone else's definition of your 'needs'.

Do you really *need* the things that the advertisers want you to buy, for example – whatever their true cost? Each one is manufactured at a cost to the environment; a cost which ultimately comes back to you since you are a part of that environment.

Many of us buy these things because we are persuaded that they will fill a gap in our souls. They won't, of course. What will fill that gap is to stir our spirits with an energy that is life-affirming and healthy.

Ask yourself where 'away' is. When we throw things 'away', where do they go? Sometimes to landfills where some of it, like plastics, will not degrade for a thousand years. Sometimes it is dumped at sea or ends up there. The UN Environment Program estimates that on every square mile of our oceans, there are 46,000 pieces of plastic litter. Around a million seabirds and 100,000 seals, sea lions, whales, dolphins, and sea turtles choke on it every year.[63] And yet, what we call rubbish could often be used by someone else or recycled for our own use. A brief pause for thought might suggest something more positive you could do with the things you no longer want before you throw them 'away'.

Teach your children well. Shamans have always known that the decisions we make today, and everything we show and tell our children, will have an impact not just now or tomorrow but for *seven generations* to come.

Even if those who think they are in charge of our planet today have not been taught how to love or shown the beauty of nature, we can do better and teach our children well so they can become nature's allies and better leaders than our own.

Teachers could take their children out to the fields, so they can see and feel the presence of nature and, with guidance, come to understand that everything is precious, has spirit, and is worthy of love, instead of just hearing about nature and its 'resources' in a classroom which keeps them removed from it and teaches them that the world is a commodity.

Parents could spend time with their kids in nature. If you have children, you could involve them in herb planting, gathering and preparation, or creating a medicine garden. Children are naturally gifted at tuning in to plants and can often tell you things about their spirits that are as surprising as they are brilliant.

History has shown us time and again that our fate should not be left to governments or to a mythical 'someone else'. If we care about our lives, our children, and our planet, we need to take back power for ourselves and find our own solutions.

In reality, this is no more than loving nature in return for the love and healing it so graciously gives to us – and loving ourselves enough to care.

Being alive requires only one thing of us: that we remember who we are and our origins in the stars.

To be an effective healer is to open our hearts to nature while we blaze, on our evolutionary pathways, like fire across the skies. Then we will remember the most important thing of all: that while we live, our purpose, like that of all gods, is to love.

> The fire divine in all things burning
> Seeks the mystic heart anew,
> From its wanderings far again returning
> Child, to you.
> **George Russell,** *Benediction*

EXPLORATIONS: RETURNING THE LOVE OF THE PLANTS

> Come heart, where hill is heaped upon hill
> For there the mystical brotherhood
> Of sun and moon and hollow and wood and river and stream
> Work out their will.
> **William Butler Yeats,** *Into the Twilight*

This last exploration is simple: Journey, meditate, and reflect.

Ask yourself what it *means* that your are a child of God.

What does it mean to be a god? To know that you began life in the stars and that we are all – you included – descended from one consciousness which is vast, intelligent, loving, and divine?

What would a god do, in this world right now, with your life?

In other words, if you *truly* believed in your divinity; that a part of the universe burned within your soul; and that God had trusted the Earth to you, what would *you* do?

What healing and wisdom are you capable of as God's expression here, and how will you use your gifts?

I think you will be amazed at all the ways you will find to use your natural and God-given talents and to allow your star to burn brightly in this world.

Take a journey to where "hill is heaped upon hill" and join "the mystical brotherhood".

In that place of "sun and moon and hollow and wood and river and stream", what is *your* will?

GLOSSARY

Abred: The physical world; God manifest

Adfyd: 'Reworld' – a state of vision and Grace where we become ecstatically aware of the presence of God in every aspect of our lives

Afallon: Avalon, the mystical Isle of Apples

Amanita muscaria: Fly agaric, a visionary 'plant of the gods'

Anam cara: The 'soul friend' who will listen to us with sympathy and without judgement, and support us no matter what

Atonement: *At-One-Ment*; the practice of making amends for our actions so that our souls come back to balance

Awen: The Celtic Otherworld or land of spirit

Awenyddion: "Awen-inspired Ones"; diviners who delivered their prophecies and diagnoses in verse

Axis mundi: The World Tree, cosmic axis, or centre of the world

Bards: Inspired poets

Bile: In Ireland, a Holy place marked by one or more sacred trees

Blessing: A transference of energy or good spirit in response to a petition or prayer

Cernunnos: Lord of the Animals and Leader of the Wild Hunt

Confession: The process of speaking aloud, openly and honestly, about the problems we face or the things we have done which do not rest easy on our souls

Cunning man/woman: A folk healer and spiritual herbalist

Dagda, The: "The Good God"; High King of the Tuatha De Dannan, and the Supreme God in Irish mythology

Dieting: A practice for building a connection to the spirit of a particular plant by careful attention to rituals surrounding food, drink, and sexual and other activities

Druids: Priests, healers, and magicians

Elements: Air, Earth, Fire, and Water, the four energies which must be present in the body and in balance to ensure good health.

Through them we attain the fith element: Spirit

Entheogen: A plant "which causes an individual to become God-like". A teacher or visionary plant

Eolai: Spiritual guide

Faeries: Spirits of the Earth. To some, the souls of sinners who were not evil enough for hell and not good enough for heaven and who are now caught between worlds, awaiting Judgement Day when their sins will be forgiven. To others, gentle creatures, known as the People of Peace or The Gentry

Faery doctors: Plant healers who work with herbs and spirits to create cures

Fly agaric: *Amanita muscaria*, a visionary plant of the gods

Fogou: An underground ceremonial structure for religious rituals and the initiations of shamans. The name is derived from *fogo*, the Cornish word for cave

Frith: A Scottish divinatory technique

Fritheir: A Scottish diviner or seer

Gazing: A shamanic practice where the eyes are allowed to go out of focus so that the energy field of a patient can be clearly seen

Grace: The experience of the numinous, the sensation of being in the presence of God or receiving His blessings and gifts

Green man: Foliate masks which depict plants taking the form of men – or men becoming plant-like

Hollow hills: Celtic burials mounds, often the home of faeries

Icaros: Magical chants or songs received from or offered to plant spirits

Illness as a metaphor: A term invented by Susan Sontag to suggest that the nature of any illness is related to the nature or personality of the sufferer

Immrama: Irish tales of heroic voyages to spirit lands

Invocation: A prayer or appeal intended to lead to a manifestation of spirit

Lucifers: Light-bringers or Angels of Light

Magic mushroom: Psilocybe. A visionary plant of the gods

Mag Mell: The Delightful Plain. One of the realms of spirit; a land where there is no sickness, aging, or death, and where happiness lasts forever

Medsen fey: In Haiti, a 'leaf doctor' or shamanic herbalist

Nemeton: A grove of sacred trees, ruled by Nemetona, the goddess of the grove

Offerenda: A ritual offering to honour nature and the spirit of the plants

Ogham: The language of the trees, the ancient alphabet of the Celts

Ovates: Omen-readers and future-seers

Placitas: A "heart-to-heart, soul-to-soul" consultation, similar to confession

Plant of vision: A power or teacher plant which acts as a master guide and tutor to the shaman. Often entheogenic

Psilocybe: 'Magic mushroom'. A psychotropic visionary plant of the gods

Psychopomp: The shamanic soul-escort who guides the deceased into the world of spirit. To the Welsh, personified as Ankou

Rathadach: An omen of good luck

Rosadach: An omen of bad luck

Scrying: A divinatory technique which looks for signs in candle flames or reflective surfaces to reveal the past and future

Shamanic journey: A state of trance consciousness which allows a healer to enter the world of spirit

Sheela na Gig: Carvings of naked women displaying exaggerated genitalia, often found over the doors and windows of churches in Wales and Ireland. Symbols of power and fertility, they are also said to protect against magic, evil spirits and death

Sidhe: The People of the Mounds; spirit allies and healers

Sin: An intrusive energy that can leave the mind, emotions, body, and soul depleted

Sin eaters: "Devourers of human sin". Healers (originally Welsh) who remove 'sin' (intrusive energy) from the souls of their patients

Sitheans: 'Hollow hills'. Burial mounds which are often the home of faeries

Soma: In the *Rig Veda*, a plant described as a god. According to some writers, fly agaric (*Amanita muscaria*) is a strong candidate for the legendary "Irish Soma"

Soul loss: The loss of life force as a result of trauma, shock, or abuse

Spirit extraction: A shamanic healing process for removing intrusive spirits or energies which are unhealthy and not our own

Spirit intrusions: Unhealthy energies which find their way into our energy system

Teacher plant: A plant of extraordinary power which acts as a master tutor and guide to the shaman-healer or his patient

Tuatha De Dannan: In Irish and Scottish mythology, the people of the goddess Danu, who arrived in Ireland on May 1 (Beltane), descending on dark clouds. Originally from the four northern cities of Falias, Gorias, Murias and Finias, they were admired and feared for their legendary skills of magic and warriorship

Turasaiche: 'One who journeys to spirit'; a shaman

Turas: A pilgrimage to make observances at a Holy place

Urtication: Flogging the body with nettles as a form of healing to remove intrusive energies

World tree: Metaphorically, the tree which stands at the centre of the world and connects the realms of spirit and man

INDEX

REFERENCES AND BIBLIOGRAPHY

Introduction

1. For more on this Celtic creation myth see J Williams (Ab Ithel), *The Barddas of Iolo Morganwg* Vol. I, (Longman & Co. 1862)

2. EA Holmes, quoting Kenneth Morris, the Welsh poet-philosopher, in *As Old as Time* (published in Sunrise magazine, November 1976, Theosophical University Press)

3. Taliesin, *The Mabinogion*, Translated by Ronald Stuart Thomas. Taliesin (c534-c599) is the earliest poet of the Welsh language whose work has survived. His name is associated with the *Book of Taliesin*, a book of poems that was written down in the Middle Ages (around 1275).

4. J Williams (Ab Ithel), *The Barddas of Iolo Morganwg*, (Longman, 1862)

5. John Aubrey, *Remains of Gentilism and Judaism* (1688)

Chapter 1

6. Bertram Puckle, *Funeral Customs: Their Origin and Development* (1926)

7. Anton Szandor LaVey (1930-1997) was the founder and High Priest of the Church of Satan, an important part of the human potential movement of the 1960s. Anton LaVey's book *The Satanic Bible* is published by Avon 1969. LaVey was influenced by the works of philosophers Friedrich Nietzsche and Ayn Rand, and believed that freedom and personal expression, and the responsibility that comes with it, are essential to human life and that people have the right to choose their own beliefs and destinies. For LaVey, Satan is not a literal deity any more than God, but a metaphor for natural impulses.

8. *The Holy Bible,* New Testament. First published in 1582 by the English College at Rheims; revised and annotated in 1749 by Bishop Richard Challoner.

9. The Catholic Encyclopaedia is available online at

http://www.newadvent.org/cathen/14004b.htm

10. James Lovelock, *Gaia: A New Look at Life on Earth*, (Oxford University Press, 2000)

11. *The Story of the Fairy Rowan Tree* – see www.sacred-texts.com/neu/celt/kis/kis55.htm

12. The Celtic wheel of the year, or tree calendar, see www.the-tree.org.uk

13. Robert Graves, *The White Goddess: A Historical Grammar of Poetic Myth*, (Farrar, Straus and Giroux, 1966)

Chapter 2

14. John Pughe (tr.), *The Physicians of Myddfai: Ancient Herbal and Other Remedies Associated with a Legend of the Lady of the Lake*, (Felinfach, Llanerch, 1993)

15. Ralph Waldo Emerson and Larzer Ziff, *Nature and Selected Essays*, (Penguin Classics, 2003)

16. *Tribal cures for modern ailments*, Saturday, 28 August, 1999, at http://news.bbc.co.uk/1/hi/world/americas/431829.stm

17. Jo Nevill, *Ancient secrets of plants' miracle cures unravelled in the laboratory*, The Observer newspaper (published in the UK, Sunday August 21, 2005)

18. If you know any other traditional plant remedies, the scientists at Kew Gardens would like to hear from you. You can email them at m.simmonds@kew.org

19. Alexander Carmichael, *Carmina Gadelica: Hymns & Incantations*, (Floris Books, 1997)

20. Traditional folklore tale of Jack Fox and the Leprechaun

21. Alfred Vogel, the Swiss naturopath, in his book, *Geshundheits Nachrichten*. Extracted in *Health Way* magazine, archived online at http://www.healthywaymagazine.com/Issue42/the_nature_doctor.html

22. One medsen fey… [p56]

23. Richard Folkard, reprinted as *Plant Lore, Legends, and Lyrics: Embracing the Myths, Traditions, Superstitions, and Folk-lore of the Plant Kingdom*, (Cornell University Library, 1969)

24. David Hoffmann, *Welsh Herbal Medicine*, (Abercastle Publications, 1978)

Chapter 3

25. see http://www.mayoclinic.com/health/garlic/NS_patient-garlic

26. Doris Lentz, in *Plant Spirit Shamanism: Traditional Techniques for Healing the Soul*, by Ross Heaven, (Destiny Books, 2006)

27. For more information on Nux vomica, visit http://abchomeopathy.com/r.php/Nux-v and for information on lovage, see http://www.botanical.com/botanical/mgmh/l/lovage42.html

28. William Butler Yeats, in John Sharkey, *Celtic Mysteries: The Ancient Religion*, (Sanas Press, 1993)

29. Lady Augusta Gregory, *Visions and Beliefs in the West of Ireland* (First published 1920. Reprinted by Colin Smythe Ltd, 1992)

30. John O'Donahue, *Anam Cara: A Book of Celtic Wisdom*, (Harper Collins, 1998)

Chapter 4

31. Myles Dillon, *The Cattle Raid of Cooley*, in *Early Irish Literature*, (Four Courts Press, 1994)

32. In the account that Valentine Greatrakes wrote of his life, which was published in 1666 under the wonderful title, *A Brief Account of Mr Valentine Greatrakes and Divers of the Strange Cures by Him Lately Performed. Written by Himself in a Letter Addressed to the Honourable Robert Boyle, Esq.*

33. A W Moore, *The Folk Lore of the Isle of Man: Being an Account of its Myths, Legends, Superstitions, Customs & Proverbs*, (D Nutt, 1891)

Chapter 5

34. David Hoffmann, *Welsh Herbal Medicine*, (Abercastle Publications, 1978)

35. Barry Cunliffe, *Iron Age Communities in Britain: An Account of England, Scotland and Wales from the Seventh Century BC until the Roman Conquest*, (Routledge & Kegan Paul, 2005)

36. Joseph Campbell, *The Power of Myth* (Anchor Books, 1991)

37. Caitlin Matthews, *Mabon and the Mysteries of Britain: An Exploration of the Mabinogion* (Arkana, 1998)

38. Anthony Weir, *Irish Sweathouses and the Great Forgetting*. Expanded from articles in *Archaeology Ireland*, Vol 3, issue 1, 1989, and *The Ley Hunter*, issue 119, September 1993. Available online at www.irishmegaliths.org.uk

39. John Matthews, *Taliesin: Shamanism and the Bardic Mysteries in Britain and Ireland*, (Aquarian Press, 1991)

40. Katharine Briggs, A *Dictionary of British Folk-tales in the English Language*, (Routledge & Kegan Paul, 1970)

41. G J Davies, *Touchyng Witchcrafte and Sorcerye*, (Dorset Record Society, 1985)

42. Christina Hole, *A Mirror of Witchcraft*, (Chatto & Windus, 1957)

Chapter 6

43. Elizabeth Andrews, *Ulster Folklore* (Reprint of 1913 Elliot Stock edition, by EP Publishing, 1977)

44. *British Goblins: Welsh Folk-lore, Fairy Mythology, Legends and Traditions* by Wirt Sikes, can be viewed online at http://arthursclassicnovels.com/arthurs/fairy/goblin10.html

45. Michael J Harner, ed, *Hallucinogens and Shamanism*, (Oxford University Press, 1973)

46. Peter Lamborn Wilson, *Irish Soma*, in Psychedelic Illuminations 1(8), 1995

47. Thomas Riedlinger, *Fly-Agaric Motifs in the Cú Chulaind Myth Cycle*. Lecture given at the Mycomedia Millennium Conference as published on www.Erowid.org. October 29 1999 (Published by Erowid, June 2005)

48. R Gordon Wasson *Soma: Divine Mushroom of Immortality*, (Harcourt Brace Jovanovich, 1968)

49. Peter Lamborn Wilson, *Ploughing the Clouds: The Search for*

Irish Soma, (City Lights, 1999)

50. Jean Markale, *The Celts: Uncovering the Mythic and Historic Origins of Western Culture*, (Inner Traditions, 1993)

51. Sir Richard Colt Hoar, *Journal of a Tour in South Wales*, (1793)

52. Francisco A. Moreno, MD, Pedro Delgado, MD, Alan J Gelenberg, MD, *Effects of Psilocybin in Obsessive-Compulsive Disorder*, (University of Arizona, 1990)

53. E J Mundell, *'Magic Mushroom' Drug Study Probes Science, Spirituality.* (HealthDay News, Tuesday July 11, 2006)

54. John Lilly, *The Center of the Cyclone*, (Three Rivers Press, 1985)

55. There is more information on kava at www.erowid.org. Kava and other teacher plants, are available from suppliers including Deva Ethnobotanicals at www.salvia-divinorum-supplies.co.uk

Chapter 7

56. Erin Everett, *Plant Healing, Fire Wisdom: New Life Journal interviews author and teacher Eliot Cowan*, June/July 2003. The full interview can be read online at http://www.newlifejournal.com/junjul_03/cowan_07_03.shtml

57. Echinacea studies reported in BBC News, *Echinacea 'can prevent a cold'*, June 25, 2007. Online at http://news.bbc.co.uk/1/hi/health/6231190.stm.

58. Susan Sontag, *Illness as Metaphor*, (Farrar Straus & Giroux, 1988)

59. Christine Scallan, *Herbal Cures: Healing Remedies from Ireland*, (Newleaf, 2003)

Chapter 8

60. The fungus known as the Old Man of the Woods is now being taken seriously in cancer research. See, for example, S Tomasi, F Lohézic-Le Dévéhat, P Sauleau, C Bézivin, and J Boustie, *Cytotoxic activity of methanol extracts from Basidiomycete mushrooms on murine cancer cell lines*, 2004.

61. Sean O' Suilleabhain, the head of the folklore department at University College Dublin, quoted in Patrick Logan, *Irish Folk Medicine,* (Appletree Press, 1999)

62. Trefor M Owen, *Welsh Folk Customs* (National Museum of Wales, 1968)

63. See Kenneth R Weiss, *Plague of Plastic Chokes the Seas,* published in the Los Angeles Times, August 2, 2006. Available online at http://www.latimes.com/news/printedition/la-me-ocean2aug02,0,5274274,full.story

64. William Butler Yeats (13 June 1865 – 28 January 1939) was an Irish poet awarded the Nobel Prize in Literature. The Nobel prize-giving committee said: "he always inspired poetry, which in a highly artistic form gives the expression of the spirit of a whole nation." His works include *The Tower* (1928) and *The Winding Stair and Other Poems* (1929).

BIBLIOGRAPHY

Niall Mac Coitir, *Irish Trees: Myths, Legends & Folklore* (Collins Press, 2003)

Jane Gifford, *The Celtic Wisdom of Trees: Mysteries, Magic and Medicine*, (Godsfield Press, 2000)

Ross Heaven, *Plant Spirit Shamanism: Traditional Techniques for Healing the Soul*, (Destiny Books, 2006)

Ross Heaven, *The Way of The Lover: Rumi and the Spiritual Art of Love*, (Llewellyn, 2007)

Ross Heaven, *The Sin Eater's Last Confessions: Lost Traditions of Celtic Shamanism*, (Llewellyn 2008)

Caitlin Matthews, *Mabon and the Mysteries of Britain: An Exploration of the Mabinogion* (Arkana, 1998)

Caroline Myss, *Why People Don't Heal and How They Can*, (Three Rivers Press, 1998)

Claire Nahmad, *Garden Spells*, (Gramercy, 1999)

George William Russell (A.E.), *The Candle of Vision: Inner Worlds of the Imagination* (Prism Press, 1990)

W Jenkyn Thomas, *The Lady of the Lake*, from *The Welsh Fairy Book* (includes the story of *The Physicians of Myddfai*)

ABOUT THE AUTHOR

Ross Heaven is a therapist and healer, and the director of The Four Gates Foundation, one of Europe's leading organisations for the teaching, promotion, and application of spiritual wisdom and freedom psychology.

He offers courses and retreats in healing, self-awareness, and indigenous wisdom, including plant spirit workshops of particular relevance to this book. www.thefourgates.com/ for details.

He also hosts spiritual journeys to sacred landmarks in Ireland, and to work with the indigenous healers and plant shamans of the Peruvian Amazon and Andes.

He is the author of ten books, including: *Plant Spirit Shamanism: Traditional Techniques for Healing the Soul, The Sin Eater's Last Confessions: Lost Traditions of Celtic Shamanism, Love's Simple Truths: Meditations on Rumi and The Path of The Heart,* and *The Way of The Lover: Rumi and the Spiritual Art of Love.*

Infinite Journeys, a trance drumming tape to accompany the shamanic journeys described in these books, is also available from the Four Gates website: www.thefourgates.com.

DEDICATIONS AND THANKS

For my children, Jodie, Mili, Ocean, and Javan.

DISCLAIMER

The techniques, recipes, and approaches in this book are for interest purposes only.

The exercises presented here have been tested in many real-life applications and no harm has ever arisen, but it is important that you proceed with caution and take responsibility when pursuing these practices. Double-check all formulas and recipes for legality and safety before you use them internally or externally, and if you are in any doubt, take medical or other advice to reassure yourself that there are no contraindications.

Any application of these exercises is at the reader's own risk, and the author and publisher disclaim any liability arising directly or indirectly from them or from the recipes described herein.

BOOKS

O is a symbol of the world, of oneness and unity. In different cultures it also means the "eye," symbolizing knowledge and insight. We aim to publish books that are accessible, constructive and that challenge accepted opinion, both that of academia and the "moral majority."

Our books are available in all good English language bookstores worldwide. If you don't see the book on the shelves ask the bookstore to order it for you, quoting the ISBN number and title. Alternatively you can order online (all major online retail sites carry our titles) or contact the distributor in the relevant country, listed on the copyright page.

See our website **www.o-books.net** for a full list of over 500 titles, growing by 100 a year.

And tune in to myspiritradio.com for our book review radio show, hosted by June-Elleni Laine, where you can listen to the authors discussing their books.

MySpiritRadio

SOME RECENT O BOOKS

The Celtic Wheel of the Year
Celtic and Christian Seasonal Prayers
Tess Ward

This book is highly recommended. It will make a perfect gift at any time of the year. There is no better way to conclude than by quoting the cover endorsement by Diarmuid O'Murchu MSC, "Tess Ward writes like a mystic. A gem for all seasons!' It is a gem indeed.
Revd. John Churcher, Progressive Christian Network

1905047959 304pp **£11.99 $21.95**

Daughters of the Earth
Goddess Wisdom for a Modern Age
Cheryl Straffon

Cheryl combines legend, landscape and women's ceremonies to create a wonderful mixture of Goddess experience in the present day. A feast of information, ideas, facts and visions.
Kathy Jones, co-founder of the Glastonbury Goddess Conference and author of *The Ancient British Goddess*

1846940163 240pp **£11.99 $21.95**

Goddess, the Grail and the Lodge
Alan Butler

Utterly absorbing, this is a wide-ranging book. From the Rosicrucians to the Golden Thread, from the Astrology of Washington to the architecture of Rosslyn Chapel, from the Magdalene to Parzival, and a whole lot more - it's all in here, clearly and economically written and logically set out.

To anyone with the slightest interest in these areas, I highly recommend this excellent book.
Kate Gooch, Editor, *Avalon Magazine*

1903816696 360pp **£12.99 $15.95**

The Gods Within
An interactive guide to archetypal therapy
Peter Lemesurier

When I saw "The Gods Within", I had to pick up the book. This text includes a personality diagnostic, made up of keywords describing various personality traits. Using this easy to use system, the reader then finds out which Greek God or Goddess archetype that he or she most needs to explore. Ten main personality types are thoroughly described with a number of subcategories slightly modifying each. The reader is then encouraged to explore and embrace this archetype through a series of exercise: self-enquiry, invocation, meditation, and remedial activities.
Dr Tami Brady, TCM Reviews

1905047991 416pp **£14.99 $29.95**

Healing Power of Celtic Plants
Angela Paine

She writes about her herbs with such a passion, as if she has sat all day and all night and conversed with each one, and then told its story herein. She has hand picked each one and talks of its personality, its chemistry, magic, how to take it, when not to take it! These herbs and plants are of this land, grown out of our heritage, our blood and sadly almost forgotten. I love this book and the author. It's a great book to dip into.
Trish Fraser, Druid Network

1905047622 304pp **£16.99 $29.95**

Living With Honour
A Pagan Ethics
Emma Restall Orr

This is an excellent pioneering work, erudite, courageous and imaginative, that provides a new kind of ethics, linked to a newly appeared complex of religions, which are founded on some very old human truths.
Professor Ronald Hutton, world expert on paganism and author of *The Triumph of the Moon*

9781846940941 368pp **£11.99 $24.95**

Maiden, Mother, Crone
Claire Hamilton

Conjures the ancient Celtic Triple goddess in rich first-person narratives that bring their journeys to life. The greatest gift offered is Hamilton's personification of the goddesses' experience of pain, ecstasy and transformation. She brings these goddesses to life in such a powerful way that readers will recognize remnants of this heritage in today's culture.
SageWoman

1905047398 240pp **£12.99 $24.95**

Medicine Dance
One woman's healing journey into the world of Native...
Marsha Scarbrough

Beautifully told, breathtakingly honest, clear as a diamond and potentially transformative.
Marian Van Eyk McCain, author of *Transformation Through Menopause*

9781846940484 208pp **£9.99 $16.95**

Shamanic Reiki
Expanded Ways of Workling with Universal Life Force Energy
Llyn Roberts and Robert Levy

The alchemy of shamanism and Reiki is nothing less than pure gold in the hands of Llyn Roberts and Robert Levy. Shamanic Reiki brings the concept of energy healing to a whole new level. More than a how-to-book, it speaks to the health of the human spirit, a journey we must all complete.
Brian Luke Seaward, Ph.D., author of *Stand Like Mountain, Flow Like Water, Quiet Mind, Fearless Heart*

9781846940378 208pp **£9.99 $19.95**

The Heart of All Knowing
Awakening Your Inner Seer
Barbara Meiklejohn-Free

A 'spell' binding trip back in time. It's a rediscovery of things we already knew deep down in our collective consciousness. A simple-to-understand, enjoyable journey that wakes you up to all that was and all that will be.
Becky Walsh LBC 97.3 Radio

9781846940705 176pp **£9.99 $24.95**

The Last of the Shor Shamans
Alexander and Luba Arbachakov

The publication of Alexander and Luba Arbachakov's 2004 study of Shamanism in their own community in Siberia is an important addition to the study of the anthropology and sociology of the peoples of Russia. Joanna Dobson's excellent English translation of the Arbachakov's work brings to a wider international audience a fascinating glimpse into the rapidly disappearing traditional world of the Shor Mountain people. That the few and very elderly Shortsi Shamans were willing to share their

beliefs and experiences with the Arbachakov's has enabled us all to peer into this mysterious and mystic world.
Frederick Lundahl, retired American Diplomat and specialist on Central Asia

9781846941276 96pp **£9.99 $19.95**

The Other Side of Virtue
Where our virtues really came from, what they really mean, and where they might be taking us
Brendan Myers

This is one of the most important books you can read. 'The Other Side of Virtue' explores territory that is vitally important to understand at this critical time in our history. Reading it will deepen your soul. It might seem strange to recommend cheating when discussing a book on virtues and ethics, but let me say this: this is one of the most important books you can read, but if you doubt this, turn to the very last two pages of the book and read the final passage marked 'The Messenger'. Better still, start at the beginning and let the book deepen your soul and broaden your understanding.
Philip Carr-Gomm, author of *Sacred Places*, Chief of the Order of Bards, Ovates and Druids

9781846941153 272pp **£11.99 $24.95**

The Way Beyond the Shaman
Birthing a New Earth Consciousness
Barry Cottrell

"The Way Beyond The Shaman" is a call for sanity in a world unhinged, and a template for regaining a sacred regard for our only home. This is a superb work, an inspired vision by a master artist and wordsmith.

Larry Dossey, MD, author of *The Extraordinary Power Of Ordinary Things*

9781846941214 208pp **£11.99 $24.95**

Walking An Ancient Path
Rebirthing Goddess on Planet Earth
Karen Tate

At last, a book about The Goddess for those of us who happily dwell in the twenty first century! This is a thoroughly modern and practical look at the different aspects of goddess worship and how it can be integrated into the modern world. It could bring about a major change in our under-standing of the Goddess. Karen Tate's book is a must have. It deserves an important place on the bookshelves of anyone with a curiosity about the world's oldest religion. A truly stunning effort.

Dharma Windham, author of *Reluctant Goddess*

9781846941115 416pp **£11.99 $24.95**

Adjust Your Brain
A Practical Theory for Maximising Mental Health
Paul Fitzgerald

Fascinating, enthralling, and controversial. Paul Fitzgerald's theories of brain functioning and mental illness are certain to capture the attention of the lay person and the esteemed scientist alike. Regardless of your opinion of his ideas, this book is certain to do one thing: make you think very deeply about your perceptions, your emotions, your moods, and the very nature of what it is to be human...and about our abilities to alter these through the use of psychopharmacology.

Dr. Ryan K. Lanier, PhD, Behavioral Pharmacologist, Johns

Hopkins University School of Medicine

978-1-84694-0 224pp **£11.99 $24.95**

Developing Spiritual Intelligence
The Power of You
Altazar Rossiter

This beautifully clear and fascinating book is an incredibly simple guide to that which so many of us search for: the kind of spiritual intelligence that will enable us to live peacefully, intelligently, and joyfully whatever our circumstances.
Dr Dina Glouberman, author of *Life Choices, Life Changes*

1905047649 240pp **£12.99 $19.95**

Don't Get MAD Get Wise
Why no one ever makes you angry!
Mike George

After "The Power of Now", I thought I would never find another self-help book that was even a quarter as useful as that. I was wrong. Mike George's book on anger, like a Zen master's teaching, is simple yet profound. This isn't one of those wishy-washy books about forgiving people. It's just the opposite....a spiritually powerful little book.
Marian Van Eyk, *Living Now Magazine*

1905047827 160pp **£7.99 $14.95**

Is There an Afterlife?
David Fontana

It will surely become a classic not only of parapsychology literature in general but also of survival literature in particular.
Radionics
Winner of the Scientific and Medical Network prize

1903816904 496pp **£14.99 $19.95**

Back to the Truth
5000 years of Advaita
Dennis Waite

This is an extraordinary book. The scope represents a real tour de force in marshalling and laying out an encyclopaedic amount of material in way that will appeal both to the seasoned and to the introductory reader. This book will surely be the definitive work of reference for many years to come.
Network Review

1905047614 600pp **£24.95 $49.95**

Everyday Buddha
Lawrence Ellyard

Whether you already have a copy of the Dhammapada or not, I recommend you get this. If you are new to Buddhism this is a great place to start. The whole feel of the book is lovely, the layout of the verses is clear and the simple illustrations are very beautiful, catching a feel for the original work. His Holiness the Dalai Lama's foreword is particularly beautiful, worth the purchase price alone. Lawrence's introduction is clear and simple and sets the context for what follows without getting bogged down in information... I congradulate all involved in this project

and have put the book on my recommended list.
Nova Magazine

1905047304 144pp **£9.99 $19.95**

Everything is a Blessing
David Vennells

I've read a few self-help books in my time, but this is the only one I've ever talked about with no reserve or irony. Vennells charmed me utterly with his open enthusiasm, simple presentations of deep spiritual truths, suggestions for achievable goals and workable plans and doable exercises. It leaves readers with the feeling of having been spoken to directly by someone who genuinely cares about them and wants to help them heal and succeed.
Marion Allen fiction site

1905047223 160pp **£11.99 $19.95**

Mysticism and Science
A Call for Reconciliation
Swami Abhayananda

A lucid and inspiring contribution to the great philosophical task of our age – the marriage of the perennial gnosis with modern science.
Timothy Freke author of *The Jesus Mysteries*

184694032X 144pp **£9.99 $19.95**

One Self
Philip Jacobs

Philip Jacobs has explained the almost inexplicable idea of "Oneness" probably as clearly and accessibly as is possible here, and without religious bias. Recognising the need for a metaphorical approach to illuminate this esoteric concept, he is liberal with his use of helpful parables and anecdotes from many sources, ancient and modern. He explores topics such as consciousness, identity, suffering, happiness, love, freedom and meaning, and I particularly liked the chapter on illness. He has provided an all round summary for anyone new to, or renewing a path of spiritual growth.
Pilgrims

1905047673 160pp **£9.99 $19.95**

Ordinary Women, Extraordinary Wisdom
The Feminine Face of Awakening
Rita Marie Robinson

This will become a milestone in female spirituality. Not only does it recount the fascinating and intimate stories of twelve 'ordinary' women in their search for peace and self knowledge, the author engages the reader with her own quest through her integrity, vulnerability and courage. Beautifully written with captivating honesty, this unique book will become an inspiration for both men and women alike, also looking for the essence of who they truly are.
Paula Marvelly, author of *Teachers of One*

9781846940682 256pp **£11.99 $24.95**

Practicing Conscious Living and Dying
Stories of the Eternal Continuum of Consciousness
Annamaria Hemingway

This is a glorious book. A science of immortality is in the making, and Annamaria Hemingway is one of its architects.
Larry Dossey, MD, author of *The Extraordinary Healing Power of Ordinary Things*
9781846940774 224pp **£11.99 $24.95**

Suicide Dictionary
The History of Rainbow Abbey
Paul Lonely

This is a startlingly original work of sheer genius – highly recommended, if you can handle it.
Ken Wilber, author of *The Integral Vision*

9781846940613 176pp **£7.99 $16.95**

Take Me To Truth
Undoing the Ego
Nouk Sanchez and Tomas Vieira

"Take Me To Truth" is not just a book - it's a revelation. Nouk Sanchez is a gifted spiritual teacher who knows what she is talking about and has a good idea of how to communicate her knowledge. The writing of Nouk and Tomas is uncompromising, exciting and strikingly consistent.
Gary R Renard, author of *The Disappearance of the Universe*

978-1-84694-0 256pp **£9.99 $19.95**

The Barefoot Indian
The Making of a Messiahress
Julia Heywood

The book is warm, funny, but altogether life changing. It teaches lessons that are infinitely valuable, on life itself and the nature of the cosmos and the ailments of the human race. They are so many answers, and my old self is itching to show off and tell you some, but I am not able to. The book is one you must journey through and reflect upon by yourself. A touching and life changing read, "The Barefoot Indian" is definitely one to pick up the next time you visit your local bookstore. It is an easy and essential read for all ages.
She Unlimited Magazine

1846940400 112pp £7.99 $16.95

The Bhagavad Gita
Alan Jacobs

Alan Jacobs has succeeded in revitalising the ancient text of the Bhagavad Gita into a form which reveals the full majesty of this magnificent Hindu scripture, as well as its practical message for today's seekers. His incisive philosophic commentary dusts off all the archaism of 1500 years and restores the text as a transforming instrument pointing the way to Self Realization.
Cygnus Review

1903816513 320pp **£12.99 $19.95**

The Good Remembering
A Message for our Times
Llyn Roberts

Llyn's work changed my life. "The Good Remembering" is the most important book I've ever read.
John Perkins, NY Times best selling author of *Confessions of an Economic Hit Man*

1846940389 196pp **£7.99 $16.95**

You Are the Light
John Martin Sahajananda

To the conventional theologian steeped in the Judaeo-Christian tradition, this book is challenging and may even be shocking at times. For mature Christians and thinkers from other faiths, it makes its contribution to an emerging Christian theology from the East that brings in a new perspective to Christian thought and vision.
Westminster Interfaith

1903816300 224pp **£9.99 $15.95**

The Celtic Wheel of the Year
Celtic and Christian Seasonal Prayers
Tess Ward

This book is highly recommended. It will make a perfect gift at any time of the year. There is no better way to conclude than by quoting the cover endorsement by Diarmuid O'Murchu MSC, 'Tess Ward writes like a mystic. A gem for all seasons!' It is a gem indeed.
Revd. John Churcher, Progressive Christian Network

1905047959 304pp **£11.99 $21.95**